GREGOR MALANTSCHUK

THE CONTROVERSIAL KIERKEGAARD

translated by
Howard V. Hong
and
Edna H. Hong

The Kierkegaard Monograph
Series

edited by
Alastair McKinnon

A widespread misapprehension of Søren Kierkegaard is
that his concern for the individual and the individual's
relation to the divine excluded any significant attention
to social and political problems. In this volume Gregor
Malantschuk, before his death one of the world's foremost Kierkegaard scholars, demonstrates the social
dimension of Kierkegaard's thought—the relation between the individual and the state, the distinctive and
complementary character of man and woman, his possible acquaintance with Marxist thought. The book
shows Kierkegaard as an astute observer of the social
and political situation of his time and underscores the
differences between his presuppositions and those of
the present day. The book is a translation of *Den kontroversielle Kierkegaard* together with two additional
essays by Malantschuk.

Gregor Malantschuk is the author of Kierkegaard's
Thought. *Howard and Edna Hong have edited and
translated* Søren Kierkegaard's Journals and Papers,
volumes 1-7. Howard Hong is Editor-in-Chief of
Kierkegaard's Collected Works.

The Kierkegaard Monograph Series

edited by
Alastair McKinnon

Gregor Malantschuk

THE
CONTROVERSIAL
KIERKEGAARD

translated by
Howard V. Hong
and
Edna H. Hong

Wilfrid Laurier University Press

Translated from
Den kontroversielle Kierkegaard
Copyright © 1976 by Gregor Malantschuk, Copenhagen
Translation copyright © 1980 by Howard V. Hong
Published by
Wilfrid Laurier University Press
Wilfrid Laurier University
Waterloo, Ontario, Canada
N2L 3C5

Canadian Cataloguing in Publication Data

Malantschuk, Gregor.
The controversial Kierkegaard

(The Kierkegaard monograph series)
Translation of Den kontroversielle Kierkegaard.

ISBN 0-88920-093-9 bd.

1. Kierkegaard, Søren, 1813-1855. I. Title.
II. Series.

B4377.M31813   198'.9   C80-094521-2

Cover design by Mary Wagner

Contents

Editor's Introduction ix

Preface xiii

1. Political and Social Aspects of
   Kierkegaard's Thought 1

2. The Relevance of *Fear and Trembling* 18

3. Kierkegaard's View of Man and Woman 37

4. Assumptions and Perspectives 62

5. Did Kierkegaard Read Karl Marx? 76

Editor's Introduction

One of the various aims of the Kierkegaard Monograph Series is to give English-speaking readers access to some of the best secondary literature on Kierkegaard now appearing in Scandinavia and, particularly, Denmark. The first volume was a translation of Ib Ostenfeld, *Søren Kierkegaards Psykologi* (Rhodos, 1972), and the present one is of Gregor Malantschuk, *Den kontroversielle Kierkegaard* (Vinten, 1976), together with two related studies which Dr. Malantschuk has kindly provided for this edition.

The central theme and focus of the original work is Kierkegaard's social and political thought and the new material ("The Relevance of *Fear and Trembling*" and "Assumptions and Perspectives") contributes directly to this theme. Recognizing and underscoring this unity, I have therefore inserted these pieces as chapters 2 and 4 of the present edition. Thus, the present first three chapters treat an aspect of Kierkegaard's thought in some depth, the fourth provides the general background of these views, and the fifth deals with a related interesting historical question.

Kierkegaard is often dismissed as an unworldly, conservative, or even merely "religious" thinker. The present book shows these estimates to be profoundly mistaken. The first chapter clearly shows that he was an astute observer of the social and political situation of his time, demonstrates the depth and profundity of his social and political views, and boldly underscores the differences between his presuppositions and those of our own materialistic age. The second shows the permanent and deeper significance of *Fear and Trembling*, insists upon the necessity of the primacy of the individual over the state, and demonstrates the importance of this principle for the just and right ordering of society. The third ascribes a distinctive and complementary character to man and woman, reveals the subtlety of Kierkegaard's views on the relation of the sexes, and shows that he has thought much more deeply about this question than many of our very vocal contemporaries. The fourth provides an overall view of Kierkegaard's thought in the light of which we can better understand his position on these and other social issues. The fifth is a kind of appendix dealing with the question of the probable extent of Kierkegaard's knowledge of Marx and arguing that he must have read one of the latter's small pseudonymous articles entitled ''Luther as Judge between Strauss and Feuerbach.'' However, Kierkegaard has his own vision and anyone looking for ''influences'' will be disappointed.

The first chapter of the present book was originally delivered as a lecture at the University of London in 1974 and with the present third and fifth chapters comprised the original *Den kontroversielle Kierkegaard*. The second chapter was presented at a meeting of the *Søren Kierkegaard Selskabet* in 1975 but has not been previously published in any form. The fourth chapter is a revision of material which appeared originally in Danish as Dr. Malantschuk's Introduction to an edition of *Om min Forfatter-Virksomhed* and related material (Copenhagen, 1963). None of this material has been previously published in English.

Before his lamented death in August, 1978, Dr. Malantschuk was regarded as one of the world's outstanding Kierkegaard scholars. It is both a pleasure and an honour to present these reflections to a wider public and I am extremely grateful to him for making them available for this series. Incidentally, in accordance with his custom, the references to the *Samlede Værker* are to the first edition.

It is a pleasure to record my thanks to the distinguished translators Howard and Edna Hong for their translation of this work and for supplying most of the appropriate English references.

I am pleased also to record my thanks to the Danish *Statens humanistiske Forskningsraad* for assistance in connection with the expenses of the translation from Danish into English.

This book has been published with the help of a grant from the Canadian Federation for the Humanities, using funds provided by the

Social Sciences and Humanities Research Council of Canada. I hereby express my thanks to both of these organizations.

February, 1979   Alastair McKinnon

Preface

As a thinker, Søren Kierkegaard was concerned with humanity's most central existential problems. Therefore, he also sought answers to such important questions as a person's relation to society and politics and the relation between the sexes.

Kierkegaard's honest and original treatment of these subjects is based on a penetrating knowledge of the presuppositions of the human mind and spirit. Consequently it is of value to become acquainted with what Kierkegaard has to say on these questions, and it is especially pertinent in an age when everything is opened to debate and confusion seems to prevail.

Since Kierkegaard in his view of mankind places the main emphasis on the spiritual, his thoughts invariably arouse conflict, insofar as it is material and earthly happiness that people are primarily seeking. But this very controversial aspect of Kierkegaard can be the occasion for a testing and investigating of one's own philosophy of life.

As far as I can make out, it will be Kierkegaard's wide-ranging, down-to-earth, and consistent thinking to which men must turn in the future in order to cure the rootlessness of the age and in order to find a new point of departure for their own life and for their relation to their fellow beings.

Gregor Malantschuk

1

Political and Social Aspects of Kierkegaard's Thought

• It is rather common knowledge that Søren Kierkegaard is called the father of existential philosophy because he gave impetus to this modern philosophical direction. Kierkegaard's influence on modern theology and psychology is also well known. But it is not so well known that Kierkegaard's authorship gives evidence of continuous attention to political and social questions.

Before going further into this subject, we must mention an essential and important presupposition for all of Kierkegaard's activity both as a person and as an author. He perceived very early that he was an exception, an extraordinary,[1] born at the beginning of a crisis period of unsuspected world-historical dimensions. Very early he saw it as his task to enter into the issues of the age and to try to find

---

[1] See *Søren Kierkegaard's Journals and Papers*, ed. and tr. Howard V. Hong and Edna H. Hong, I-VII (Bloomington: Indiana University Press, 1967-78; Don Mills, Ontario: Fitzhenry & Whiteside), vol. I, no. 1081 [hereafter *JP* I 1081] (X² A 180). See also *JP* VI 6497 (X² A 45); *Søren Kierkegaards Papirer*, I-XI³ (Copenhagen, 1909-1948), 2d ed. photo-offset with supplemental vols. XII-XIII (1969-70), vol. IX A 64 [hereafter (X² A 180) in conjunction with *JP* and *Papirer* IX A 64 in references to *Papirer* only]; *The Point of View for My Work as an Author* (New York: Harper, 1962), pp. 79-80 (*Samlede Værker*, I-XIV, 1st ed., Copenhagen, 1906 [hereafter *SV*], XIII 566).

possible ways of surmounting the crisis. In many journal entries, Kierkegaard states that he was especially fitted for this task and had been given the necessary talents and qualifications.

In 1837 Kierkegaard's teacher and close friend Professor Poul Martin Møller wrote an article in which he predicted the coming "catastrophes" threatening western culture because it had lost its Christian foundation. Poul Møller maintained that when men lose their relation to the eternal and faith in the immortality of the soul, the human personality will undergo a drastic devaluation. As a consequence, men end up in nihilism.[2] In all likelihood, Poul Møller discussed this question with Kierkegaard, inasmuch as they had close contact with each other at the time and had many conversations.[3]

Kierkegaard's journals from this period[4] also reveal that he was actively working with the same problems as Poul Møller and that he was aware of the political and social consequences of the impending nihilism and the resulting levelling of all values. It was perfectly clear to Kierkegaard that the deepest cause of the crisis was religious in nature.

In his very first book, *From the Papers of One Still Living*, which came out in 1838, the year Poul Møller died, Kierkegaard considered the problems that would arise from the levelling of values. On the one side, Kierkegaard shows how this levelling will manifest itself, and on the other he indicates the only basis for a positive development. Levelling will make men feel a steadily increasing need to find support in organizations, general assemblies, etc. as they more and more lose faith in the worth of the individual person. Thus they will try to make up in quantity for what they have lost in quality. Kierkegaard ironizes over the "ant hills" that will be built, where the decisive factor is how many there are.[5] In such a situation, political life gradually becomes more and more unstable as its foundation further disintegrates.

From the outset, the positive basis and starting point, to which Kierkegaard refers even in his first book, is concentration on the responsible individual human being, "the single individual"[6] [*den*

---

[2] *Efterladte Skrifter af Poul M. Møller*, I-VI (3d ed.; Copenhagen, 1855-56), V, pp. 52-53.
[3] See Uffe Andreasen, *Poul Møller og Romantismen* (Copenhagen, 1973), pp. 86-87.
[4] See *JP* V 5116 (I B 2), 5181 (I A 328).
[5] *SV* XIII 63-64 [*From the Papers of One Still Living*].
[6] Ibid.

Enkelte]. The category of "the single individual" is studied from every possible existential point of view and thereby becomes central to Kierkegaard's whole authorship.

It is of interest to note that in this same book Kierkegaard indicates the two principal types of the single individual, namely, the single individual within the human sphere and the single individual in relation to Christianity. But for both of these types it holds true that in order to become the single individual a person must first of all realize the insufficiency and uncertainty (fraudulence) of the purely temporal. Only then can a person relate to the eternal truth, which is the positive condition for becoming the single individual.

Commencing in 1838 and for a period of two years, Kierkegaard was totally engaged in his theological studies and made only very few and sporadic comments on politics. In one of them he stated: "In many ways the Church Fathers' descriptions of demons fits the politicians of our day. They lived in the air (they are far too windy to be able to keep their feet on the ground); they lived on the smoke of *offerings* and *incense*; they were very mobile and *could pass over the whole world in a hurry.*"[7]

Before completing his final university examination in theology in 1840, Kierkegaard began the preliminary work for his doctoral dissertation on *The Concept of Irony with Constant Reference to Socrates*. It was not accidental that Kierkegaard chose Socrates as the subject of his dissertation. He was strongly captivated by Socrates' personality and acknowledged a close spiritual relationship to this ancient classical figure.[8] Socrates, too, had lived in a period of crisis. The Greek mythology that was the original religious foundation for Greek culture had lost the power of its convictions and had to be replaced by something higher. Socrates' problem was likewise the bewildered crowd that let itself be influenced by demagogic politicians. According to Kierkegaard, Socrates also was primarily interested in the single individual, whom he taught to seek the truth within himself and not in externalities. By concentrating on Socrates, Kierkegaard learned a great deal about politics and the individual's relation to the state. Socrates broke through the authority of the state as the highest court. His ironic attitude to all external powers relativized all the laws of the state. Socrates pointed instead to the "infinity" that is inside every man and should be a person's highest authority.

---

[7] *JP* IV 4093 (II A 436).
[8] See *JP* VI 6839 (X⁵ A 104).

Kierkegaard, too, used this Socratic irony as the point of departure for his own views on society. In other words, social and political life is relative by nature. It is not proper to elevate it to the absolute. The absolute is to be found only in the inner man. It is not anything external. Man, of course, must obey external authorities, but there is the possibility of conflict between the external powers and a person's inner conviction. In that case, man must act according to his conscience. This viewpoint, which burst forth with Socrates, signified a revolution in the ancient world's view of the relation of the individual to the state and society. But of course it was clear to Kierkegaard that Christianity, too—only on a higher level—had the same view of man's relation to all earthly laws and powers.

In *The Concept of Irony*, Kierkegaard uses Socrates to show the individual's hard-won independence from externals and from the state. But in this book he does not as yet show how an individual who has won his independence can once again relate positively to the state and thereby to society and politics. This comes first in the pseudonymous book *Either/Or*, the book that begins Kierkegaard's authorship proper. In the first part of this work, Kierkegaard's pseudonym gives examples of people who as yet have not won a positive relation to the eternal but in various ways remain suspended in the sphere of multiplicity. A section of part one of *Either/Or* is entitled "The Rotation Method," with the subtitle "An Essay on the Theory of Social Prudence." It is a parody of the situations resulting in society when petty and calculating prudence alone prevails.

In part two of *Either/Or*, the pseudonymous writer Judge William makes an interesting and strong attempt to draw his social and political views into an organic, consistent overall view. Through Judge William, Kierkegaard introduces a plan for ethical action that comprehends the political and the social as well. An important component of this plan is the personal ethic of which Socrates is claimed to be the representative. Thus Socrates here is no longer considered solely as an ironist but also as an ethicist. But Judge William's plan is based mainly on what Christianity teaches about "duties towards God, towards one's self, and towards one's neighbor"[9]—a division into a religious, a personal, and a social-civil ethic. Therefore, Kierkegaard does not have Judge William come up with anything

---

[9] *Either/Or*, I-II (Princeton: Princeton University Press, 1971), II, p. 270 (*SV* II 238).

new. What is new is Kierkegaard's use of these three main premises to clarify human action and thereby to illuminate concretely the goals of human life within the various existential stages. It is Kierkegaard's view that men should order their lives in these three lines of direction if they are to develop toward the goals God has set for human life.

These three lines of direction must always correspond with each other lest men end up being narrow, warped, and biased. The relation to God has highest priority. This relation must always have an absolute character. On the next level is a person's relation to himself. This means that men must seek to form themselves into ethical persons. On the third level is a person's relation to the external world, primarily to his fellow men. The shape of this relation is again dependent on a person's view of his fellow men. The pagan saw his fellow man as a member of the body politic or the group, whereas the Christian always sees the other as his neighbour.

In harmony with these three lines of direction, we can speak of a person as a "religious self," "a personal self," and "a social, a civic self."[10] Kierkegaard very strongly accentuates—especially in his upbuilding literature—the personal line as he simultaneously insists upon the relation to the absolute. In so doing, Kierkegaard tries to avoid the danger inherent in the age, namely, an over-emphasis on the political and the social, since he holds them to be relative in character. Indeed, the goal—as the pseudonymous writer Johannes Climacus later expresses it—is "The Simultaneous Maintenance of an Absolute Relation to the Absolute Telos and a Relative Relation to Relative Ends."[11] By accentuating the individual and the personal in relation to God instead of to the social and political, Kierkegaard continually places more stress on the meaning of personhood, expressed finally in the formulation of his most important category, "the single individual."

In his writing, especially in the pseudonymous works, Kierkegaard describes very precisely how one becomes a single individual. Everyone begins as a particular being [*Individ*], that is, as Kierkegaard sees it, as totally dependent upon heredity and environment. It takes strain and struggle to become a responsible and independent person. One must make the leap from the esthetic to the ethical stage. Here a person enters into relation to the eternal, which is the begin-

---

[10] Ibid., p. 267 (*SV* II 235).
[11] *Concluding Unscientific Postscript* (Princeton: Princeton University Press, 1941), p. 347 (*SV* VII 335).

ning of becoming the single individual. The pseudonymous writers describe the collisions one must experience in order to become the single individual. An individual cannot actually be said to have become the single individual until he enters into a personal, existential relationship to God as the eternal. This takes place in the religious stage. This movement is a movement of freedom. A person is not required to make this movement but can very well stay in the esthetic stage all his life. But if he does, he actually sinks to a still lower stage and becomes a "particular instance, a specimen" of the human race.[12] But specimen men are very quickly converted into mass-men.

After having dealt with the dialectic of the single individual with respect to the esthetic, the ethical, and the religious in such important works as *The Concept of Anxiety, Philosophical Fragments, Stages on Life's Way*, and *Concluding Unscientific Postscript*, Kierkegaard turns again to the spiritual crisis in society that threatens to devaluate the single individual. He goes more deeply into the ideas about the political and the social already touched on in his first book, *From the Papers of One Still Living*. His book *Two Ages*[13] gives a very exhaustive and detached analysis of the approaching era, of which Poul Møller used the term "nihilism."[14] Kierkegaard himself uses the expression "leveling,"[15] thereby indicating clearly that the coming age would be most characterized by a disintegration of all higher values, and that this would be a long process.

In this book, Kierkegaard vigorously emphasizes that the cause of the crisis is religious. He scrupulously delineates the various symptoms of the crisis. One of the most significant symptoms is that men no longer act as individuals but become ciphers, functioning as the public or the irresponsible mass. Speaking of the "public," he says: "The public is everything and nothing, the most dangerous of all powers and the most insignificant: one can speak to a whole nation in the name of the public and still the public will be less than one single actual human being, however unimportant."[16] Kierkegaard points

---

[12] *JP* II 2024 (X² A 489); *The Point of View*, p. 111 (*SV* XIII 593). See also *JP* II 2048 (XI¹ A 42), 2049 (XI¹ A 60).

[13] *Two Ages: The Age of Revolution and the Present Age: A Literary Review* (Princeton: Princeton University Press, 1978), pp. 68-110 (*SV* VIII 64-102).

[14] See *Efterladte Skrifter*, V, pp. 88, 101. The expression is later used particularly by Turgenev, Dostoevsky, and Nietzsche.

[15] *Two Ages*, pp. 84-96 (*SV* VIII 79-89).

[16] Ibid., p. 93 (*SV* VIII 87).

out further that when men are no longer enthusiastic over the eternal values, which are the only values worth being enthusiastic over, they eventually are taken over by finite reflection and sink to becoming mass-men. But this signifies simultaneously a great step backward in man's development. The step *forward*, according to Kierkegaard, is in "the development of individuality"[17] in such a way that the significance of the single individual becomes even more decisive. Although Kierkegaard stresses very strongly that men must become single individuals, he nevertheless concedes that "the principle of association"[18] also has some significance, thus recognizing the legitimacy of associations for the advancement of material interests. In fact, he later declares that "in relation to all temporal, earthly, worldly matters, the crowd may have competency, and even decisive competency as a court of last resort."[19] In other words, Kierkegaard concedes the legitimacy of majority decisions when they pertain to relative, practical matters—but not when they concern ethical and religious decisions. But since the crisis of the age is ethical-religious in character, it can never be solved with the help of "the masses," but only by the single individual, for whom the eternal is a matter of earnestness. Outside a relation to the eternal, particular individuals are nothing more than vanishing shapes in the world-historical process.[20]

Having analyzed the age in *Two Ages*, Kierkegaard concentrates more and more on the upbuilding literature. It is characteristic that Kierkegaard dedicates the first part of his next book, *Upbuilding Discourses in Various Spirits*, to "That Single Individual" in order to indicate clearly his position on the age's enthusiasm for the "numerical"[21] and the quantitative.

Kierkegaard's journal entries from these years reveal that he is closely watching the social and political currents in Denmark and in the rest of Europe. He is especially interested in the communistic movements. He fears that they will exploit the masses for their own

---

[17] Ibid., p. 106 (*SV* VIII 99). S.K. also calls this process "individuation." *JP* II 2024 (X² A 489).

[18] *Two Ages*, p. 106 (*SV* VIII 99).

[19] *The Point of View*, p. 110 (*SV* XIII 592).

[20] See *Postscript*, p. 485 (*SV* VII 475). Poul Møller had already expressed himself in a similar manner. See *Efterladte Skrifter*, V, p. 72.

[21] *Two Ages*, p. 106 (*SV* VIII 99). S.K. uses this expression very often in his journals, along with the phrase "the crowd." On this, see *The Point of View*, pp. 112, 138 (*SV* XIII 593, 612), as well as *JP* IV 4852 (IX A 4).

ends, because they play upon the most concrete and elemental needs of men, namely, their economic and social needs. From his journal entries about the "bread-uprisings" in Europe, it appears that he saw clearly that they were the start of new social and political revolutions. In this he finds confirmation that he was right in emphasizing the category of "the single individual." He writes: "It all fits my theory *perfectly*, and I dare say it will come to be seen how *exactly* I have understood the age . . . ."[22] Concurrently, Kierkegaard maintains that the communistic movements will not be satisfied with specific political and social reforms. Quite apart from specific economic and philosophical assumptions, they also attempt to solve men's ethical and religious problems and in a way totally different from Kierkegaard's way of solving these problems.

There were especially two main points in communism against which Kierkegaard had to protest. First, its denial of God, its atheism. Second, its claim that external distinctions between men can be equalized to produce economic and social equality.

With regard to the first point, Kierkegaard carefully demonstrated that the existence of God can never be proved or disproved scientifically. This question is completely outside the competence of science. At the same time, Kierkegaard tried to demonstrate in his writings that all human life dissolves into meaninglessness if a person loses the relation to the eternal.

As to the second point, Kierkegaard believed it to be fraudulent to speak of the fulfillment of the principle of equality, since it will never be possible to establish equality in this world, the very nature of which is dissimilarity. The danger in these communistic currents was that along with atheism and the principle of equality they would mobilize the uncritical masses.

In the same year that Kierkegaard mentioned the "bread-uprisings," he finished the book *Works of Love*. Whereas earlier he had focused his attention on the ethical and religious development of the single individual, he now takes up the issue of "sociality,"[23] that is, the ethics that has to do with the relation to the other person, to the neighbour. This book is deliberately against communism's social and political tendencies. Here Kierkegaard discusses the ideal of equality and is not sparing in his arguments that it is impossible "completely to

---

[22] *JP* IV 4116 (VIII¹ A 108); see also *JP* VI 6017 (VIII¹ A 172).
[23] *JP* V 5972 (VIII¹ A 4).

produce worldly equality.'' There will always be differences among men with respect to capabilities, predispositions, and external contributing factors. These differences can never be totally abolished. According to Kierkegaard, only ''the equality of the eternal''[24] can be attained. By this he means that every person possesses something that is higher than anything of this world, namely, the possibility of the eternal, and that all men are on an equal footing in the relation to God.

Kierkegaard also calls to account men's attempt to set God aside and put man in God's place. Of the consequences of that, he says: ''And now, as a reward for such presumption, men will come closer and closer to transforming all existence into doubt or confusion.''[25] In addition, Kierkegaard points out how to halt this kind of ''insurrection against God'' or ''mutiny,'' as he calls it. ''I wonder if every individual is not duty-bound towards God to stop the mutiny . . . not by domineering and wanting to force others to obey God, but by unconditionally obeying and thereby expressing for his part that God exists and is the only master, and that he, on the other hand, is unconditionally obedient to him?''[26]

In *Works of Love*, Kierkegaard also discusses multiple human relations and, from the Christian point of view, suggests solutions. Even though only one of the chapters states directly that it is ''rightly turned against communism,''[27] it nevertheless is true of the whole book that in addition to providing Christian norms it is polemically directed against communism.

It is interesting that *Works of Love* came out the same autumn in which Marx and Engels undertook the task of drawing up the *Communist Manifesto*, published in February of the following year. With this, *Works of Love* stands as a program script for a view of life diametrically opposed to what is expressed in the *Communist Manifesto*.[28]

Kierkegaard's polemic against the mass man, the crowd, and the one-sided accent on class distinctions is intensified after the February

---

[24] *Works of Love* (New York: Harper, 1962), p. 83 (*SV* IX 73).

[25] Ibid., p. 120 (*SV* IX 112).

[26] Ibid., pp. 121-22 (*SV* IX 114).

[27] *JP* IV 4124 (VIII¹ A 299).

[28] Karl Löwith in *From Hegel to Nietzsche* (New York: Holt, Rinehart, and Winston, 1964), p. 151, says that Kierkegaard in his *Two Ages* has created an Anti-Communist Manifesto. It is more accurate to say that this came later with *Works of Love*.

Revolution in 1848. In one of the entries from this time, Kierkegaard says the following about communism:

The idea of equality will be regarded as up for debate; equality has now become a question discussed throughout Europe.

Consequently every one of the older forms of tyranny will now be powerless (emperor, king, nobility, clergy, even money-tyranny).

But another form of tyranny is a corollary of equality—fear of men. I have already called attention to this in the last discourse of "The Gospel of Suffering." I called attention to it again in the third part of *Christian Discourses*, no. 6.[29]

Of all the tyrannies, it is the most dangerous, in part because it is not directly obvious and attention must be called to it.

The communists here at home and other places fight for human rights. Good, so do I. Precisely for that reason I fight with all my might against the tyranny of the fear of men.

Communism ultimately leads to the tyranny of the fear of men (just see how France at this moment is suffering from it); right here is where Christianity begins.

What communism makes such a big fuss about, Christianity accepts as something which follows of itself, that all men are equal before God, therefore essentially equal. But then Christianity shudders at this abomination which wants to abolish God and create fear of the crowd of men, of the majority, of the people, of the public.[30]

In the journal entries from 1848, we find the most numerous and the most detailed comments on the coming crisis. It is very significant that Kierkegaard now uses for the first time, and very often, the word "catastrophe" for the crisis, the word Poul Møller also used. He speaks of "the European catastrophe of the current year" and believes that it is only an "introduction."[31] A time is coming when it will be possible to manipulate everything by way of the crowd. "Everything will revolve around getting the crowd in shoes and then to get the balloting, shouting, torch-carrying, and armed crowd on one's side, irrespective, totally irrespective, of whether it understands anything or not."[32] The crowd is always ready for the "decision of upraised hands or the fists upraised for battle."[33] For the crowd

---

[29] *The Gospel of Suffering* (Minneapolis: Augsburg, 1948), pp. 138-64 (*SV* VIII 398-416); *Christian Discourses* (Princeton: Princeton University Press, 1971), pp. 228-38 (*SV* X 222-32).

[30] *JP* IV 4131 (VIII¹ A 598).

[31] *Papirer* IX B 10, pp. 308-10.

[32] *Papirer* IX B 24, p. 326.

[33] Ibid., p. 324.

consists of zeroes that can be used for whatever is to be without responsibility on the part of the crowd, for only the single individual as the single individual can have responsibility. Spiritually the single individual is much stronger than the crowd, a fact that Kierkegaard regards as a paradox. In this connection, what one of the pseudonymous writers says in another context is appropriate: "But one should not think slightingly of the paradoxical."[34]

In Kierkegaard's opinion, the qualitatively new will begin in this paradoxical way with the single individual. The crowd can never create anything qualitatively new.[35] But the single individual can fulfil his task only by accepting ridicule and suffering, and in that connection Kierkegaard, especially in his last years, touches on the question of martyrdom.

So Kierkegaard takes a very critical attitude toward communism. Yet he did not know it in the form Marx and Engels gave to it and in which it thereafter marched victoriously around the world. Kierkegaard had only heard about socialist theoreticians such as Proudhon.[36] But, as far as I can see, Kierkegaard's view of communism would not have changed in the slightest had he known it in the form Marx and Engels gave to it—quite the contrary. There he would have encountered the idea of atheistic communism carried to its extreme with the help of specific philosophical and sociological theories. The contrast between Kierkegaard's own position and that of Marxist communism would have emerged in all its sharpness. Kierkegaard would have been even more strongly convinced that in

---

[34] *Philosophical Fragments* (Princeton: Princeton University Press, 1962), p. 46 (*SV* IV 204).

[35] See *JP* IV 4132 (VIII¹ A 599).

[36] Kierkegaard's familiarity with the French socialists is very likely chiefly due to discussions in the Danish newspapers, especially *Kjøbenhavnsposten*. On this, see Svende E. Stybe, *Frederik Dreier* (Copenhagen, 1959), pp. 97ff.; Anton Hügli, "Kierkegaard und der Communismus," *Kierkegaardiana*, IX (1974), 220-47. The following comment by Kierkegaard in 1849 undoubtedly refers to Proudhon's ideas on socialism: "But as a matter of fact it is the eternal that is needed. Some stronger evidence is needed than socialism's belief that God is the evil, and so it says itself, for the demonic always contains the truth in reverse." *JP* VI 6256 (*Papirer* X⁶ B 40). Cf. *JP* IV 4911 (XI¹ A 516) and editor's note.

It is interesting that as early as 1844 S.K. in all likelihood had read a little article by *Kein Berliner*, "Luther als Schiedsrichter zwischen Strauss und Feuerbach," which came out in *Anekdota* by Arnold Ruge (Zürich, 1843). *Auktionsprotokol over Søren Kierkegaards Bogsamling* (*ASKB*) 753. On this, see *Papirer* V B 1:10. *Kein Berliner* was a pseudonym of Karl Marx, which S.K. certainly did not suspect. See this volume, pp. 62-82.

the future the battle would specifically be fought between the two qualitatively opposite points of view, that is, between the Christian view of life in Kierkegaard's formulation and the communistic view of life in Marx's formulation. In both cases we have new, consistently worked-out, comprehensive views of existence and man, developed after nihilism and the devaluing of all values had undermined western culture. In our culture, a person finds himself in a spiritual void, and the question now is—which of the two views of life can eventually create stability and give life-meaning back to man. I personally believe that Kierkegaard's view of life will win out because it builds on a transcendent basis, that is, it acknowledges something higher than limited human understanding. But here it becomes a matter of choice.

Let me now try to place the central points in the new views of life face to face with each other.

For Marx, matter, the world of atoms, is primary. On the basis of this presupposition, dialectical materialism (that is, Marx's and Engels' method) attempts to give the only and ultimate explanation of existence and the issues of human life.

Kierkegaard believes in spirit—that is, in a conscious power as the presupposition for all existence.

According to Marx, the crisis in western European culture is due to the sharpening of the economic and social contrasts, to class distinctions. Marx is not primarily interested in the specific individual but in a specific social class, the proletariat. It must be organized for violent implementation of justice on earth. Religion, Christianity in particular, is regarded as a considerable hindrance in this battle, since it supposedly holds out to men an illusory reality that can only weaken the proletariat's struggle for justice. However, Marx believes that religion will disappear when the masses are properly informed about the origins of religion and its function in the class struggle, and when economic justice has been achieved. Therefore, Marx's position on religion is not neutral; on the contrary, he is very active in a battle to eliminate it.

According to Kierkegaard, the cause of the crisis is first and foremost spiritual. By abandoning the relation to the eternal, man has become bewildered and cannot find himself again as an independent being with the aid of external economic measures. Kierkegaard would call Marx's outlook on religion a "demonic religiousness."[37]

---

[37] *Papirer* X⁶ B 41.

Kierkegaard maintains that when a person attempts to root out the thought of God he destroys his own worth as a human being. He declares that "to murder God is the most horrible form of suicide, entirely to forget God is a man's deepest fall, no beast ever fell so deep as that."[38] Presumably one can kill the thought of God—but not God himself. Kierkegaard believes that no human being can escape the relation to the eternal. This will assert itself either in a positive or a negative way. Only by a positive relation to the eternal and to God will a person achieve his true destiny.

Marx, who rejects the idea of the existence of God, must of course regard man as the highest being. He says as much: "Die Kritik der Religion endet mit der Lehre, dass der *Mensch das höchste Wesen für den Menschen sei* . . . ."[39] However, this highest of beings (this man-deity) is temporary by nature, conditioned by economic factors; its goal is earthly happiness; consequently, its whole effort is spent within finiteness, and therefore within the esthetic. With this atheism, men finally end up being completely dependent on each other in a kind of social slavery, for it is faith in something higher that gives the individual person independence in his relation to other men.

It is quite clear, then, that Kierkegaard and Marx have totally different anthropologies. For Marx, mind is merely the highest product of matter.[40] Consequently Marx's anthropology is not profound. Yet he concedes that man can achieve a relative independence. Marx's strength is his penetrating knowledge of the economic factors and their significance for society. No one else has provided such a complete description of social-economic laws and of the meaning and power of capitalism. For this reason, he also understands men's struggle with economic difficulties. Thus Marx is at his best when he talks about material things and relations. But he did not make his way to a deeper insight into men's inner, spiritual struggles. He speaks of man's alienation but that alienation is conditioned by external factors.

---

[38] *Christian Discourses*, p. 70 (*SV* X 70).

[39] Karl Marx, *Frühe Schriften* (Darmstadt, 1971), I, p. 497. "The critique of religion ends with the doctrine that *man is the highest being for man.*" See *Karl Marx Early Texts* (New York: Barnes & Noble, 1971), p. 123.

[40] See Johannes Witt-Hansen, *De marxistisk-leninistiske principper* (Copenhagen, 1969), pp. 18, 80. In *Natur og Dialektik*, Engels calls man as "thinking spirit" matter's "highest flower."

Kierkegaard's anthropology, however, depicts a deeper form of alienation that is rooted in spiritual factors. Yet he does fully recognize the significance of the economic and social factors. He points out the enormous influence of heredity and environment on the individual's existence. At the same time, he firmly emphasizes that man is not a product of external factors alone. As a synthesis of the temporal and the eternal, man has the possibility of the eternal within him. With unprecedented and unparalleled precision, Kierkegaard devoted himself to man's external situations and inner conflicts. In so doing, he has given us the most penetrating explanation of man's possibilities to develop spiritually.

Marx approves of violence and violent overthrow as means for bringing about a new and just society. Kierkegaard does not believe that external changes alone can produce renewal in the form of greater justice. If men are not changed from within, all external progress will be futile. As was pointed out earlier, in *Works of Love* Kierkegaard has given the Christian orientation for living together with other men.

According to Marx, the goal for human life lies within this world. A communist society must be established, one in which the proletariat takes over all the means of production, thus abolishing class distinctions and insuring the free development of individuals.[41] Any idea of another world than this finite world is rejected as a noxious illusion.

For Kierkegaard, the ultimate goal for human life is not confined to finitude. In his opinion, no perfect society can ever be built in this world, the very essence of which, as was previously pointed out, is dissimilarity.

Marx's mode of operation, as stated earlier, is to organize mass men, the proletariat, to create the communistic society.

According to Kierkegaard, the mass man signifies a step backward in the development of the individual. He believes that the mass must first of all become single individuals who cannot be influenced by external powers or trends but who learn to obey the power that is higher than the party or the nation or any other external authority. Accordingly, it will not be manipulation of the masses and the dividing of men into classes that will lead men out of their confusion, but the single individuals who stand responsible before God. Speaking of the category of "the single individual," Kierkegaard says: "... my

---

[41] On this, see *The Communist Manifesto*, last part of section II.

whole thought activity as author is focused in this one idea, 'the single individual,' the category that will prove to be the *point de vue* of the future, the category the significance of which (politically, ethically, religiously) the future will more and more make manifest.''[42] These single individuals will know that it is impossible "to enforce complete equality," in whatever forms the equality is supposed to be established. They will teach men that "it is only religion that can, with the help of eternity, carry human equality to the utmost limit—the godly, the essential, the non-worldly, the true, the only possible human equality.''[43]

While Marx through his books was preparing for the new society—which was supposed to appear by way of violent revolution—Kierkegaard in his authorship sought to create what he calls "a new theological science of arms"[44] for the struggle to come. He speaks of a "dreadful reformation—by comparison the Lutheran reformation will almost be a jest.''[45]

So Marx and Kierkegaard confront us with two diametrically opposite and irreconcilable views of existence. As Lenin states in his book *Materialism and Empirical Criticism*, there really are only these two logical positions to choose between: materialism and idealism. With the insight of a genius, Kierkegaard already in his very first book posed these alternatives: one must *either* remain in the esthetic sphere with its demonic form of religiosity *or* make the leap into the ethical-religious sphere.

So much for the principal contrasts between Marx and Kierkegaard. In conclusion, some comments on Kierkegaard's understanding of the relation between the religious on the one side and the social and political on the other. In the preface to "Two Notes" about "The Single Individual," Kierkegaard writes: "In these times politics is everything. Between this and the religious view the difference is heaven wide (*toto coelo*), as also the point of departure and the ultimate aim differ from it (*toto coelo*), since politics begins on earth and remains on earth, whereas religion, deriving its beginning from above, seeks to explain and transfigure and thereby exalt the earthly to heaven.''[46] Here as always, Kierkegaard asserts the unconditioned

[42] *Papirer* X⁵ B 247.

[43] *The Point of View*, p. 108 (*SV* XIII 590).

[44] *JP* IV 4779 (VIII¹ A 480); see also *The Point of View*, p. 38 (*SV* XIII 539).

[45] *JP* III 3737 (XI² A 346).

[46] *The Point of View*, p. 107 (*SV* XIII 589).

dissimilarity between the political and the religious. The political—and the same holds for the social—has its goal within finitude. The religious points toward an eternal reality. These two spheres must never be confused. But the fact that they are completely dissimilar and must not be confused does not mean that they are not to interact.

In Kierkegaard's words, man must try to "translate himself"[47] from the one sphere to the other, that is, from the religious sphere to the political and social sphere. In his view, it is impossible to be gripped by the truth without its having an influence on external relations. But the external relations are specifically social and political by nature. Compared to the development that takes place in the single individual, these external affairs are relative and secondary. In these spheres, therefore, there are in fact only quantitative modifications. Therefore, it is not possible to achieve a perfect society or a perfect form of administration. It will always be a matter of something better or something worse, with everything depending on the quality of the individual.

Although Kierkegaard was very critical of communism, he would be equally critical of any form of society that would devalue the meaning and responsibility of the single individual and that would encourage arbitrariness. Therefore, Kierkegaard would not merely reject the proletariat's insurrection against God but also the insurrection of the superman and of a master race, of which Nietzsche was a representative.

Kierkegaard believed that we must always strive to create what he called the rational and organismic state. Here the administrators would not let themselves be swayed by the crowd or by fear of public opinion but would first and foremost feel responsible to the higher power. Neither must they let themselves be tempted to exploit the weakness and ignorance of their fellow men. This, of course, means that Kierkegaard was completely opposed to one person's misusing or exploiting another. He condemned cultural and class snobbery. His sympathy for the common man is also well known.[48]

In the event that responsibility breaks down and demoralization spreads, the single individual will be obliged to protest, even if he thereby exposes himself to ridicule and persecution. Kierkegaard

---

[47] *Either/Or*, II, p. 266 (*SV* II 235).

[48] For more on this, see Jørgen Bukdahl, *Søren Kierkegaard og den menige Mand* (Copenhagen, 1961).

himself did this—first by challenging *The Corsair*, Copenhagen's political-satirical paper, and later by his violent attack on the Danish state Church.

Kierkegaard has often been regarded as an unworldly, impractical, starry-eyed idealist. But he followed very closely what happened in the political and social sphere. In fact, he believed that some day there would be use for him:

> Frequently I find something sad in the fact that I, with all my capabilities, must always stand outside as a superfluity and impractical exaggeration. But the whole thing is very simple. Conditions are still far from being confused enough for proper use to be made of me. . . . But it all will end, as they shall see, with conditions getting so desperate that they must make use of desperate people like me and my kind.[49]

---

[49] *JP* VI 6709a (X³ A 680).

2

The Relevance of
Fear and Trembling

Søren Kierkegaard's book *Fear and Trembling* deals with a complex of issues in which our age has great interest, namely, the relation between the individual and society. In this slender book, Kierkegaard has succeeded not only in bringing out the many aspects of this issue but also in keenly and penetratingly depicting the challenging situations and difficult conflicts that will confront people in the society of the future as well as that of the present.

The occasion for writing this book (published in 1843) was predominantly Kierkegaard's personal problems. But it is true of Kierkegaard, as he himself said of Socrates, that "his whole life was a personal preoccupation with himself, and then Governance comes and adds world-historical significance to it."[1] That which was purely personal in these two men has been able to attain far-reaching, world-historical significance and to contain a message for other people because their personal experiences and struggles were penetrated by fundamental ethical considerations, which provide vast and universally human perspectives.

---

[1] *JP* VI 6388 (X¹ A 266); see also *Postscript*, pp. 132-33 fn. (*SV* VII 120-21).

The issue in *Fear and Trembling* centres partly in the require-
ment that the individual's desires and demands conform to society,
partly in the fact that the individual, by reason of conscience, is not
always able to acknowledge the laws of society as the highest authority, and partly (and most importantly) in the possibility that God will
demand that the individual suspend not only his own desires but also
his positive relation to society. In no other of Kierkegaard's works
are there as many examples of clashes such as these, and nowhere
else are they thrown into such clear relief as here. For this reason the
book could also be called *The Book of Conflicts*, but its title, derived
from Paul's Epistle to the Philippians,[2] indicates that the point of
origin and the centre of gravity of conflicts are primarily religious and
have to do with the personal relationship to God.

The experience that had such repercussions in Kierkegaard's life
that it gave rise to this book was his breaking his engagement and his
understanding that this was a demand from the higher power. Many
years later, in his book *For Self-Examination*, he wrote as follows—words which without a doubt refer to the breaking of his
engagement to Regine Olsen:

> Therefore, imagine someone who has fallen in love! He saw the object;
> it was in so doing that he fell in love; and this object became for him the
> delight of his eyes and the desire of his heart! and he reached for
> it—it was the delight of his eyes and the desire of his heart; he held it in
> his hand—it was the delight of his eyes and the desire of his heart! Then
> (so it goes in those old tales) he heard the command: "Let this object
> go!"

And later:

> He has to let go of that which no earthly power thinks of taking away
> from him, that which is doubly difficult to let go of, because, as you can
> well imagine, the object employs tears and pleas, implores both
> the living and the dead, both men and God, to stop him—and he is the
> one who has to let this object go! Here you have an example (if indeed he
> manages to get around that sharp corner without losing his mind) of
> what it is to die to something.[3]

---

[2] Philippians 2:12; see also *JP* III 3369 (*Papirer* II A 313) and especially 2383 (II
A 370).

[3] *For Self-Examination* (Minneapolis: Augsburg, 1940), p. 91 (*SV* XII 362); see
also *JP* VI 6473 (X⁵ A 150). Cf. Carl Jørgensen, *Søren Kierkegaards Skuffelser*
(Copenhagen, 1967), pp. 26ff.

This denotes the severity of Kierkegaard's conflict. The difficulty lay in his having to break a commitment whose fulfillment was not blocked by any external hindrances, and the issue was whether or not God would demand of a human being that he or she should break the universally human laws in order to comply with his command. In the story of Abraham's sacrifice of Isaac, Kierkegaard found a conceivable analogy to the frightful situation in which he found himself. The event on Mount Moriah then becomes the basis for the pseudonymous Johannes de Silentio's depiction in *Fear and Trembling* of not only the testing of Abraham but of the most serious ethical-religious conflicts in human existence. From this one unique conflict, he draws a variety of possible conflict situations within the various spheres of existence.

In order to elucidate the nature of the conflicts in *Fear and Trembling* and to show their significance also for our age, we must first of all examine more closely the genesis of moral and ethical concepts and then the levels of morality and ethics discussed in the book. In common with all the other concepts of existence, the ethical has many levels and many aspects. Paganism, too, has many different higher and lower forms of expression for morals and morality, while Judaism and Christianity in particular represent the highest forms of the ethical. At the same time it must be emphasized that only if one clearly distinguishes between the various levels of the ethical will one understand how serious conflicts can arise. Failure to respect the various spheres of the ethical leads only to confusion.

The fact that man on the whole can form a conception of the ethical is, according to Kierkegaard, related to his having within him an element of something eternal, something that distinguishes him from all other creatures. It is this element that is the origin of imagination or "the infinitizing reflection,"[4] as one of Kierkegaard's later pseudonyms calls it. In this way, imagination becomes the beginning of all spiritual life. But the products of the imagination must continually be subordinated to the logical element of thought as well as to the normative function of the ethical. Without this limitation there is always the danger that one will end up in the fantastic. Yet it is by means of imagination or the infinitizing reflection that a person envisions the many possibilities, some of which attract him, some of which repel him. He also discovers that he has the possibility of *being*

---

[4] *The Sickness unto Death* (Princeton: Princeton University Press, 1980), p. 31 (*SV* XI 144).

able,[5] that is, of intervening in the given actuality. This results in the individual's beginning to wish, and "for the wish there is no limit,"[6] says Kierkegaard. But out of consideration for relations to others a limit has to be set to fulfilling the wish. The establishment of such limits becomes the laws and precepts for a society, which Johannes de Silentio designates as "the universal."[7] Thus the universal establishes the relations among individuals and in this way becomes the ethic or rather the morality that applies to all in society. In certain cases it takes but a few individuals to constitute the universal. In *Fear and Trembling* the universal for Abraham consists of but "three ethical authorities"[8] whom he must take into consideration, namely, Sara, Eliezer, and Isaac. As a rule, the universal embraces large groups, such as the tribe, the nation, or the state.

The special character of the universal is that it applies to all and to every age, and in principle it ultimately embraces the whole human race. This is what Johannes de Silentio means when he declares, "The whole existence of the human race rounds itself off as a perfect self-contained sphere, and the ethical is the limitation and the fulfillment at one and the same time."[9] These two terms suggest that the universal not only sets the limit to the development of the particular individual but also supplies human existence with its goal and meaning. Since in this way it is the universal that dominates temporal life, the particular individual stands below the universal and must subordinate himself/herself to its claims.

Because the human race is constantly developing, the claims which the universal may make on particular individuals may be quite different in specific concrete cases. Judge William in *Either/Or* calls such variations within the universal "fluctuations,"[10] that is, undulations that can be caused by, for example, geographic, ethnic, or historical conditions. But however variable the universal may seem, it nevertheless always has the characteristic of making a distinction between right and wrong, between what is lawful and unlawful, and

---

[5] *The Concept of Anxiety* (Princeton: Princeton University Press, 1980), p. 44 (*SV* IV 315).

[6] *Edifying Discourses* (Minneapolis: Augsburg, 1945), III, p. 17 (ed. tr.) (*SV* IV 82).

[7] *Fear and Trembling* (Princeton: Princeton University Press, 1973), p. 128 (*SV* IV 159).

[8] Ibid., p. 121 (*SV* III 158).

[9] Ibid., p. 78 (ed. tr.) (*SV* III 117).

[10] *Either/Or*, II, pp. 267-68 (*SV* II 236).

this holds regardless of the fact that, as mentioned above, there may be great differences in what different societies regard as lawful or unlawful. With regard to this, Kierkegaard writes in 1842:

> The main point is still that one should not be diverted by the external. When, in order to subvert the position that there is an absolute in morality, an appeal is made to variations in custom and use and such shocking examples as savages putting their parents to death, attention is centered merely upon the external. That is to say, if it could be proved that savages maintain that a person ought to hate his parents, it would be quite another matter; but this is not their thought; they believe that one should love them, and the error is only in the way of expressing it. For it is clear that the savages do not intend to harm their parents but to do good to them.[11]

It is due to variations such as these that, on the whole, people in pagan societies fought their way more or less slowly to clearer and higher moral concepts. Not until Socrates did paganism arrive at the concept of the good in and for itself. Nonetheless, the lower conceptions of right and wrong also have their origin in the eternal element in man. Thus Johannes de Silentio can also call the universal "the divine," which nevertheless does not as yet cover the relationship to a personal God.

That the universal is higher than particular individuals is characteristic of paganism. Here the race, society, or the state has the right to demand everything of the individual, and thus there are many examples in paganism of nobility and self-sacrifice for the sake of society. Therefore the individual seems to attain special significance. Nonetheless, the individual person remains but a vanishing moment in the history of the race, and this is true not only in primitive paganism but in modern paganism as well.

It was especially the German philosopher Hegel who in the modern age accentuated the state as higher than individuals (which must be regarded as a step backward for Christianity), and thus it is particularly against him that Johannes de Silentio, as well as others of Kierkegaard's pseudonyms, direct their criticism. But Poul M. Møller had already declared that Hegel's philosophy rendered every rational being "but a vanishing wave in the ocean of thought."[12] It is a foregone conclusion that from this point of view the individual can only be regarded as "a speck"[13] in the development of the world, and

---

[11] *JP* I 889 (III A 202); see also *Either/Or*, II, p. 269 (*SV* II 238).
[12] *Efterladte Skrifter*, V, p. 72.
[13] *Postscript*, p. 485 (ed. tr.) (*SV* VII 475).

that the state and not the individual becomes the decisive, the essential factor.

We encounter this view of the relation between the state and the individual also in our day, especially in the countries where materialistic views of life have conquered. Under those conditions, the individual does not have the right to act as an autonomous and independent being over against society, the state, or the party. Of course, theoreticians such as Engels and Lenin believed that when the socialist state had been perfected there would come a period when the state would "wither away,"[14] and when individuals would be totally freed from the state's intervention; individuals would thereby achieve complete liberation from external powers; all that would be needed would be a form of administration for the goods and property held in common. However, this view must be labelled extremely naive and totally utopian, since it utterly disregards the truth of human nature, which will always need laws to regulate the many conflicting interests of human beings and the selfish craving of particular individuals to expand their spheres of influence. Laws force men to respect the rights of their fellow men. Without laws we undoubtedly would end up in the state of nature that Thomas Hobbes described in the sentence *"Bellum omnium contra omnes"*[15] [the war of all against all]. Thus laws and the universal will always have their crucial meaning for dealings of people with each other, and as long as the universal is ultimately traced back to the divine, it will be justified as well. Under these conditions, therefore, the individual must submit to the universal.

But at this point the question whether or not there is a higher ethic than that of the universal surfaces. It is precisely the possibility of this kind of a higher ethical norm to which Johannes de Silentio calls our attention by offering Abraham as an example. In other words, in Abraham we meet something totally new and paradoxical. Through his relationship to a personal God he stands as an individual human being higher than the human being in pagan religions and societies, for whom the universal is the highest norm. While still living totally within the universal, he obeys a higher law than the law of the universal. He has received a promise which, it is true, bears upon life within the universal; but already his obedience to a personal

---

[14] V. I. Lenin, *Staat und Revolution* (Zürich, 1934), pp. 14ff.

[15] Thomas Hobbes, *De cive*, I, 12.

God has raised him above the universal within which he lives. God's demand that he sacrifice his son Isaac signifies a testing of his obedience, but at the same time it signifies a suspension of the universal.

By using Abraham as an example, Johannes de Silentio wants to point out the deadly earnestness involved in a suspension of the universal. There is no easy transition from the relationship of obedience within the universal to the higher form of the ethical characterized by a personal relationship to God where God as sovereign Lord can demand more than the universal or any other power can demand. The greatest difficulty in the transition from the universal to the suspension of the universal by a personal relationship to God is due to the fact that while the universal is clear to everyone and all are able to understand its demands and express an opinion on them, the suspension is a private matter between God and man that takes place secretly in a person's interior being. In that case, one is responsible only to God, in whom the person believes and whom he wants to obey.

Thus Abraham undertakes the suspension, as Johannes de Silentio says, for the sake of God and for his own sake. In more detail he explains it as follows: "He does it for God's sake because God demands this proof of his faith; he does it for his own sake so that he can provide the proof."[16] Furthermore, for Abraham the difficulty of the suspension is that it was God who gave him the promise for this life within the universal, and that it is also God who demands the break with the universal. Of this contradiction Kierkegaard says: "The terrifying thing in the collision is this—that it is not a collision between God's command and man's command but between God's command and God's command."[17] But through his obedience and his faith Abraham is raised above the universal and enters the category of the absurd, which signifies that as a temporal being one acquires the quality of the eternal.[18]

In Abraham we have an example of the way a particular individual can justifiably—that is, through a personal relationship to

---

[16] *Fear and Trembling*, p. 70 (ed. tr.) (*SV* III 109).

[17] *JP* I 908 (IV B 67); cf. *JP* I 11 (X⁶ B 80).

[18] It must be noted here that there are two principal forms of the absurd (the paradox)—namely, (1) that man, who contains the possibility of the eternal by a personal relationship to God, comes within the reality of the eternal and (2) that the eternal God becomes a temporal being (Incarnation). This is the primary and essential absurdity. See *JP* III 3074 (IV C 84); *Fragments*, p. 76 (*SV* IV 226).

God—rise above the universal even though this occurs through suffering and resignation. This relationship is strengthened in an essential way in Christianity, but generally speaking it is altogether correct to say that without a relationship to a personal, transcendent power, it is impossible for a human being to rightfully maintain his independence of the universal. Abraham is, of course, the supreme example of this relationship prior to Christianity, but even in our day his example can have great relevance. It is taken for granted that the most serious conflicts in our day will focus on the extent to which the individual has a possibility for and a right to be a self, which is higher than the universal, or the extent to which the individual should conform to the universal and identify herself or himself with it. In other words, the state, the nation, or society has a rightful claim upon the individual simply because it generally holds true that the universal is higher than the particular individual.

There is something quite different about states in which the individual person is respected and one can always seek to find a balance between the wishes of the individual and the claim of the state. One can aspire to attain what Kierkegaard calls "a rational state,"[19] by which he understands a state that is an organic whole and whose laws are influenced by the Christian view of man. But we live in an age when this kind of a state is approaching disintegration. The levelling of all values and the devaluation of the meaning of the individual have marched to victory. Therefore serious collisions are inevitable—for example, if the state legalizes conduct and conditions which conflict with the individual's conscience because of his relationship to God or which he sees will have a disruptive effect upon social morality. It is with respect to this point that Johannes de Silentio in *Fear and Trembling* and Kierkegaard through his pseudonyms in other places introduce categories that can bring clarity into the confusion that prevails in our day on the issue of the relation between the state and the individual. Involved here are many important and difficult problems that will make themselves felt increasingly in the future and will demand solution.

According to Kierkegaard and his pseudonyms, there are essentially only three possibilities for a reciprocal relation between the individual and the universal. The first two have already been touched upon—namely, that the universal is above the particular individual and that the individual through his relationship to God is higher than

---

[19] *Papirer* IX B 24, p. 326.

the universal, which is the case with Abraham and to a marked degree in Christianity. The third possibility could be called the Socratic-humane and is characterized by the individual's having discovered something eternal within himself that is above all external laws. Socrates is the first representative of this point of view, and he thereby breaks through paganism's primary form, in which the centre of gravity lies within the temporal. For Socrates, his knowledge of the good in and for itself becomes the highest authority,[20] and because of this conception he stands higher than the universal even though he respects it; but he is also obliged to die for his conviction. He complies with the laws of the state only insofar as they do not conflict with his conscience, which is not based upon a "sense of shame" but upon respect for the eternal laws and the knowledge of the truth he finds in his interior self. As Kierkegaard says in *The Concept of Irony*: "In place of the sense of shame (αἰδώς), which forcefully yet mysteriously binds the individual to the reins of the state, there now appeared the decisiveness and certainty of subjectivity in itself."[21] Here a sense of shame [*Undseelse*] means fear of public opinion. Thus the individual's conscience is based upon something external—namely, the common conception of what constitutes the good.

As is known, Socrates also fought against the demoralization of the universal brought about by the ancient Sophists. Socratic humanism, however, lacked the higher mandate that Abraham had. Thus Abraham stands higher than Socrates, whom Johannes de Silentio calls "an intellectual tragic hero,"[22] whereas Abraham is called "the father of faith."[23]

However, it is first in Christianity that the single individual gets a decisive mandate to make a stand against demoralization and the misuse of power on the part of the state. The individual can get a mandate such as this only through a personal relationship to a transcendent power. This gives a person an Archimedian point that lies outside of time and space and becomes his anchor, not only in all the variables of his life in society but also in the sufferings that may be caused by taking a stand against society.

---

[20] On the same level as Socrates' knowledge of the eternal in man is Kant's formulation of the categorical imperative, which is elevated above the earthly, fluctuating laws of the state.

[21] *The Concept of Irony* (New York: Harper, 1966), p. 190 (ed. tr.) (*SV* XIII 247).

[22] *Fear and Trembling*, p. 125 (*SV* III 162).

[23] Ibid., p. 33 (*SV* III 70).

In this way the individual can come to stand higher than the universal, and in this manner, too, he will win and preserve his identity, something worthy of note in a time when so much is said about identity crisis. But it is only through a relationship to the eternal as something transcendent that a person can win his/her identity. However, as long as one regards the universal, the earthly relations, as supreme, one will never be able to attain identity with oneself. Johannes Climacus, another of Kierkegaard's pseudonyms, speaks of how difficult—indeed, how impossible—it is for the person divided among a multiplicity of earthly interests to find his deepest self. An "inhuman centipede" such as that "cannot as a matter of course be changed into an eternal identity with itself, which is the meaning of: to be the same."[24]

But the price one pays for being raised above the universal is not small. The suspension of the laws of the universal of which Johannes de Silentio speaks specifically means the simultaneous severance from absolute adherence to things of this earth. However, this suspension does not mean that one is outside the law but, on the contrary, that one submits to a higher and more severe law than that of the universal. It also presupposes, as we have seen, that there is a God; but since this can never be proved, the suspension simultaneously becomes a matter of faith in a personal God and obedience to him. Johannes de Silentio clearly distinguishes here between the ethical that is identical with the universal and is of divine origin and the ethical that rests upon a personal relationship to God. The former, as mentioned before, is found in paganism, while the latter is first found in Judaism and more particularly in Christianity. Thus Johannes de Silentio compares the suspension of the universal that Abraham has to undertake with the suspension of the universal in Christianity, where it finds its decisive expression in "the absolute duty to God." This is found, for example, in Luke 14:26: "If any one comes to me and does not hate his own father and mother and wife and children and brothers and sisters, yes, and even his own life, he cannot be my disciple."[25]

It is important to note that a legitimate suspension can only take place in and through something higher, for there is also a suspension of the universal laws that takes place on the basis of human self-will and arbitrariness. We will return to this.

---

[24] *Postscript*, p. 157 (ed. tr.) (*SV* VII 146).
[25] Cf. *Fear and Trembling*, pp. 82-83 (*SV* III 120-21).

In connection with the suspension that takes place with faith in God as the presupposition, a crucial problem arises—namely, the question of how much of his or her inner life a person in certain situations can reveal. Therefore Johannes de Silentio discusses coherently and in some detail the meaning of a person's "secrecy" and "silence," which is a live issue also in our age.

The spontaneous and immediate person begins his or her life with many wishes and desires, some of which are kept secret. But the universal requires openness of the individual and that he or she submit to all the limitations or rules that the universal or the state establishes for the development of the individual. The state wants to have full control over its subjects' enterprises, and as long as the state or society is considered to be the highest authority there is, in fact, justification for this. This control can be carried to the extreme, as we see happening within certain societies in our day. In such a case the individual does not have the right to keep matters of importance secret from the state. The state thereby takes the place of God, and obedience to it becomes the surrogate for religion. A collision is therefore inevitable if the individual has a relationship to a higher eternal power whom he feels an unconditional duty to obey. In this way the individual can come to set a limit to the power of the universal and the state.

But this kind of anchoring in a higher eternal power will lead to a totally different and higher secrecy than the secrecy of the spontaneous and immediate person. This new secrecy cannot be made intelligible to the universal, for it expresses a relationship to something eternal, and the eternal cannot be expressed directly. This secrecy, which is incommensurable with the actuality of the external, Johannes de Silentio calls silence [*Taushed*], for, unlike the secrecy of immediacy, silence is preceded by reflection and resolution.

The secrecy of immediacy always has a relative character, since it can be directly revealed, and the universal can also justifiably demand that it be abandoned. But to the degree that a person moves from the esthetic sphere to the ethical-religious, secrecy becomes a reflected silence concealing something that cannot be communicated directly. Representing the intermediate stage between relative secrecy and the higher form of secrecy is Socrates, who utilizes the interesting to draw attention to himself while his ironic behaviour conceals his deeper intentions. But Socrates does not achieve absolute silence, which is first bestowed by the personal relationship to God.

Nevertheless, Johannes de Silentio scrutinizes paganism to see if he can find an instance of someone who, like Abraham, has received from the deity a private message that will be intelligible to others and that he cannot reveal. He turns inquiringly to Aristotle's *Politics*[26] and a story of an incident in which this possibility seems to be present, since it tells of a young man who receives from the augurs a prophecy that he would have misfortune if he entered into a marriage.[27] However, Johannes de Silentio does not believe that if this prophecy came from the augurs, who were an official institution, there can be any question of a private, direct relationship to God, since it was intelligible to all that the young man had to conform to the message that the deity sent through the augurs.

After concluding his consideration of the universal within paganism, Johannes de Silentio scrutinizes the nature of the essential secrecy that can appear in Christianity and that has an absolute character. This secrecy (silence) is like Abraham's secrecy and thereby is paradoxical, for in both cases it revolves around a personal relationship to God. But instead of giving examples of a divine paradox within Christianity that is analagous to Abraham's paradox, Johannes de Silentio points out that within the Christian sphere there are also forms of a demonic paradox in which secrecy—or, more correctly, silence—is unjustified, and which appears when people in an unjustified manner break with the universal and place themselves above the laws of society.

The reason Johannes de Silentio now gives so many examples of only the demonic paradox in modern history of Christendom may be that he has discovered that there are no outstanding examples in this period of what he calls the divine paradox—that is, of the Christian faith in the eminent sense—but that on the contrary there are many examples of the opposite, the demonic paradox. That this is the case is apparent in Johannes de Silentio's sceptical attitude to the Christianity represented by the church to which he belongs. He says: "And what higher movement has time discovered since giving up entering the monastery? Is it not a paltry worldly wisdom, sagacity, faint-heartedness that sits in the place of honor, that cravenly deludes men into thinking that they have performed the highest and slyly keeps

---

[26] *Politics*, 1304 a; cf. Søren Holm, "Findes 'den religiøse Undtagelse' i Græciteten" ["Is 'the Religious Exception' Found in the Greek Mentality?"], *Kierkegaardiana*, VIII (1971), 143ff.

[27] Cf. *JP* V 5576 (IV A 8).

them from even attempting something less?''[28] It is interesting to note his sympathy for the monastic movement, which he thinks, despite its errors, nevertheless attempts to make the first step on the way to faith—namely, resignation. He goes on to say: "He who has made the monastic movement has only one movement left, the movement of the absurd." In Johannes de Silentio's view, those who in his day spoke so much about faith had not even made the movement of resignation.

Here we see Kierkegaard's pseudonym already attacking the watered-down Protestant piety that has degenerated into secularism. This is no less a live issue in our day, when the results of secularism and paganism within Protestantism and other church denominations continually become more apparent. What it actually means is that instead of a valuing of inward deepening there is a tendency towards the demonic. In one of his later journals, Kierkegaard drastically depicts one of the advanced results of this movement towards the demonic:

> In contrast to what was said about possession in the Middle Ages and times like that, that there were individuals who sold themselves to the devil, I have an urge to write a book:
>
> Possession and Obsession in Modern Times
>
> and show how people *en masse* abandon themselves to it, how it is now carried on *en masse*. That is why people run together in flocks—so that natural and animal rage will grip a person, so that he feels stimulated, inflamed, and *ausser sich* [outside himself]. The scenes on Bloksberg are utterly pedantic compared to this demonic lust, a lust to lose oneself in order to evaporate in a potentiation, so that a person is outside of himself, does not really know what he is doing or what he is saying or who it is or what it is speaking through him, while the blood rushes faster, the eyes glitter and stare fixedly, the passions boil, lusts seethe.
>
> What depth of confusion and corruption, when at the same time it is praised as the earnestness of life, as cordiality, love, yes—as Christianity.[29]

It is very significant that the first concrete example of a demonic state cited by Johannes de Silentio, namely, the merman, is drawn from the domain of the erotic. Kierkegaard saw very clearly how the erotic, the sexual, can lead a person into the demonic. In our day as well, we have seen how certain psychological theories, primarily Freud's psychoanalysis, have extensively promoted sexual liberation

---

[28] *Fear and Trembling*, p. 110 (ed. tr.) (*SV* III 148).
[29] *JP* IV 4178 (X² A 490).

as a means to greater personal development. In actuality this so-
called liberation is a movement towards the demonic in that it must be
regarded as a more or less hidden revolt against Christianity's re-
quirement of the dominion of spirit over the sensate.

Earlier, in *Either/Or*, types were portrayed who became demonic because of their obsession with the sexual—namely, Don Juan
and Johannes the Seducer—and later there are several in *Stages on
Life's Way*. But the difference between these characters and the
merman in *Fear and Trembling* lies in the way out of the demonic
with the aid of repentance, because he has met a young, innocent girl
who awakens a longing within him to begin his life over again. It is
obvious that many of the features Johannes de Silentio brings out in
his version of the legend of the merman suggest Kierkegaard's situation in his relation to Regine. The concept that receives special
emphasis in the portrayal of the merman is repentance. Only through
repentance can he be saved from the demonic. From this we see that
we are in the realm of Christianity, where we are dealing with guilt,
and where it is not resignation but repentance that is the condition for
faith.

Resignation and repentance are both forms of the movement of
infinity, but repentance is the deeper expression of this. In paganism
there could be no question of repentance in any essential sense, for
the pagan did not know a personal God. Neither did Abraham know
repentance, but this was because he was "the righteous man."[30]

Yet it is not the sexual alone that can drive people into the
demonic but also the sense of personal wrong and grievance in various forms. The focus here is on people who in one way or another feel
injured and wronged in existence, either by a higher power, by fate, or
by some external situation, and who cannot properly fight their way
out to a positive view of their hard fate and humble themselves under
it. Richard III is cited as a convincing example of this. Pitied by all for
the deformity of his body, he over-compensated for his physical
imperfection by cruelly acquiring power over others as a tyrannical
ruler. Commenting on Richard III's monologue in Shakespeare's play
The Tragedy of King Richard the Third, Johannes de Silentio says,
"His monologue in the first act of *Richard III* has more worth than all
the systems of morality, which have no intimation of the nightmares
of existence or of their explanation."[31]

---

[30] *Fear and Trembling*, p. 108 (*SV* III 146).
[31] *Fear and Trembling*, p. 115 (*SV* III 152).

I, that am rudely stamp'd, and want love's majesty
To strut before a wanton ambling nymph;
I, that am curtail'd of this fair proportion,
Cheated of feature by dissembling nature,
Deform'd, unfinish'd, sent before my time
Into this breathing world scarce half made up,
And that so lamely and unfashionable
That dogs bark at me as I halt by them.

Here we get a penetrating look into the connection between a sense of personal wrong and grievance and the demonic as the will to power.

It is striking that immediately after discussing the demonic as the result of a sense of personal wrong and grievance, Johannes de Silentio speaks of the genius's situation in existence. The explanation for this is quite simple—namely, that Johannes de Silentio believes (as does Kierkegaard) that the true genius also belongs among those who have a sense of personal wrong and grievance. Here Johannes de Silentio cites statements made by Aristotle (according to Seneca) as well as others on the genius to the effect that there is no genius who does not have a touch of madness under which he must suffer and with which he must contend.[32] Kierkegaard, too, discusses this theme in several passages in his journals. From these entries it is clear that he believes that all great geniuses have their secret suffering. The genius is commonly regarded as a highly favoured person, but the facts that the genius must pay the price for genius with melancholy and mental depression[33] and that the genius may, perhaps to a greater degree than others, be tempted to a demonic revolt against his fate are forgotten.

But the concept of personal wrong and grievance has many facets. In our day it expresses itself in one's feeling of having been wronged by the milieu in which one grew up, by the economic system, by other people, or by other social groups. This sense of grievance can be exploited by stronger personalities who are adept at manipulating people who have lost the eternal as the anchor in existence and therefore let themselves be transformed into an irresponsible mass. This is a very serious and crucial issue that needs correct solution. In *Fear and Trembling*, we do not find any solution in the sense of personal wrong and grievance as a social issue, but one can rightfully

---

[32] Seneca, *De tranquillitate animi*, 17, 10; see also *JP* I 1029 (IV A 148).
[33] *JP* IV 4599 (VIII¹ A 161); *JP* VI 6903 (XI¹ A 460); see also *JP* III 3087 (VII² B 235, p. 66).

say that Kierkegaard treats this issue in other books, where he analyzes the situations that can lead to a crisis in all spheres.[34]

In the interpretation of the character of Faust, following immediately upon the discussion of the problem of the sense of personal wrong, we see how aware Johannes de Silentio-Kierkegaard was of the coming collisions. But before going into the issues related to Faust he discusses "a similar figure"[35]—namely, an ironist. The ironist, as well as Faust, represents the intellectual-spiritual types who initiate a crisis in cultural life and thereby also a transition to a new order of things. Their irony and doubt are directed against old, obsolete social institutions, and they clear the ground in order to make room for something new. The ironist perceives the corruption of temporality and seeks the eternal, just as this became Socrates' world-historical task.

But Johannes de Silentio chooses Faust as the character who exposes the flimsy foundation upon which modern man has organized his life. He is not satisfied with irony, which is more intellectual in nature; he is a doubter, and his doubt goes deeper than irony could go,[36] for Faust's doubt has to do with Christianity. Not only does he question the truth of Christianity but primarily questions whether Christianity really and truly is the life foundation for those who call themselves Christian. Faust, in *Fear and Trembling*, confronts the question whether he should remain quiet about his doubt or express it. He knows that with his doubt he will manage "to startle and horrify men, to shake the foundations under their feet, to split them asunder, to make the shriek of alarm sound everywhere."[37] But he has sympathy for people; for this reason he ponders carefully how he can communicate his doubt without creating confusion by depriving people of their fancied security. He perceives, moreover, that he, who himself is struggling with doubt, cannot give them anything positive as a replacement. This was also Kierkegaard's own position at the time he published *Fear and Trembling*. Since that time, there

---

[34] See Two Ages, pp. 60-112 (*SV* VIII 57-105); *Works of Love*, pp. 119ff. etc. (*SV* IX 111ff. etc.).

[35] *Fear and Trembling*, pp. 116-17 (*SV* III 154 fn.).

[36] It must be noted here that Johannes de Silentio could by no means use romanticism, which is the modern form for irony, as the point of departure for his reflections on the crisis (cf. *Irony*, p. 292, fn. 2; *SV* XIII 347, fn. 2), for the romantic movement was a negative movement, whereas the character of Faust has positive elements as well.

[37] *Fear and Trembling*, p. 118 (ed. tr.) (*SV* III 155).

have been many who have been prepared to deprive people of their inherited security and faith without being able to provide a higher truth for life.

But Faust also faces the question of whether he has the right to remain quiet about what he considers to be his legitimate doubt. Thus he confronts the dilemma of either remaining quiet, thereby having "to sacrifice himself" (that is, suffer and struggle with his doubt without communicating it to anyone), or of speaking "in the awareness that he will throw everything into disorder."[38] But if he keeps quiet, his silence is unjustified, for he has a responsibility to ethics and the universal, which demand that the truth shall come out. The only way by which he can become authorized to remain silent is by becoming directly responsible to the power that is higher than the universal—or, as Johannes de Silentio says, by coming as the single individual "into an absolute relation to the absolute."[39] Thus, in using the character of Faust, Johannes de Silentio is really describing Kierkegaard's own thoughts on how he should conduct himself when he discovers that the social and ecclesiastical systems of his day rest on very shaky foundations.

But if Faust is said to be able "to get authorization for his silence" through an absolute relationship to God, then in all probability the explanation of Kierkegaard's own silence about what he called "the secret note" or "the inscription of my innermost being that interprets everything"[40] must be due to that as well. The authorization to remain silent about what "the secret note" contained must then also mean the most profound religious duty to God, and that this silence must be absolute. The probability of this conjecture is strengthened by the fact that the contents of the very next journal entry[41] after the one about the secret note have a strong resemblance to the contents of the sentences in *Fear and Trembling* that follow upon the discussion of authorization. Consequently, Kierkegaard understood his life to be as if "under divine confiscation." It could never become *publici juris*[42] [public property], which meant that he had received a private order from God that he was to be used in a special service. This he later expressed as follows:

---

[38] Ibid., p. 120 (ed. tr.) (*SV* III 157).
[39] Ibid.
[40] *JP* V 5645 (IV A 85); here "note" most probably should be taken to mean communication, information, command.
[41] *JP* II 2111 (IV A 86).
[42] *Fear and Trembling*, p. 87 (*SV* III 125).

From the very beginning I have been as if under confiscation, and every moment I have sensed that it was not I who played the master but that it was another who was the master, have sensed it with fear and trembling when he let me realize his omnipotence and my nothingness, sensed it with indescribable blessedness when I committed myself to him and the task in unconditional obedience.[43]

Bearing these things in mind, one can understand Kierkegaard's subsequent severe attack on the pastor and theologian A. P. Adler, who believed that he had had a revelation but whose garrulousness about it demonstrated just the opposite. Adler did not understand that in such a circumstance absolute silence is required, whereas Kierkegaard, after having received "the secret note," became "a person who, with a life dedicated in holy resolution, works in complete silence."[44] As "the true extraordinary," Kierkegaard struggled to find and to give a positive answer to the difficult problems of the future and, as we know, in the course of the next years provided a map of the road that could lead to a renewal. Thus his doubts about, and his denunciation of, his contemporary age, on which Johannes de Silentio had already passed judgment in *Fear and Trembling*, did not come to the forefront until many years later in the church conflict.

Johannes de Silentio's Faust merely hints at the approaching crisis; in our day the crisis itself speaks its own clear language. In *Fear and Trembling*, we can read that only an adherence to the ethical and religious requirements can show us the way out of the crisis. Human ideals, as well as Christian ideas, must stand out clearly in all their purity and unconditionality. Ultimately, however, respect for these ideals can be maintained only by faith in a personal God, who is the reality that is higher than all human knowledge and capability and whose activity, therefore, seen from the angle of the human intellect, must be regarded as paradoxical and absurd. Thus it is a fallacy to speak of going beyond faith and thinking that one can replace faith with philosophic knowledge. That was what Hegel attempted to do in his philosophic system, and in our day many others have tried in like manner to "cleanse" faith with the aid of scientific knowledge—for example, by a demythologizing process. Johannes de Silentio would have repudiated all these attempts, inasmuch as they cannot help the individual in his deepest existential conflicts.

---

[43] *The Point of View*, p. 69 (ed. tr.) (*SV* XIII 559).
[44] *Papirer* VII² B 235, p. 67; see pp. 61-67.

Not until a person has perceived that he/she cannot cope with existence by one's own powers and endeavours does he or she have the possibility to come to the faith that Johannes de Silentio designates as the highest human passion. But to the person who does not manage to get that far, but who nevertheless is honestly struggling, he says: "But also the person who has never arrived at faith has enough tasks for his life, and if he loves these honestly his life will not be wasted, even if it is never comparable to the lives of those who perceived and grasped the highest."[45]

As a book of conflicts, *Fear and Trembling* is of contemporary relevance not only in a time of crisis such as ours; it will always be of contemporary relevance, for it deals with the essential conflicts in human life. Kierkegaard himself expected a great deal from this book. Several years after its publication, as late as 1849, he wrote of it: "O, once I am dead, *Fear and Trembling* alone will be enough for an imperishable name as an author. Then it will be read, translated into foreign languages as well. The reader will almost shriek from the frightful pathos in the book."[46]

---

[45] *Fear and Trembling*, p. 131 (ed. tr.) (*SV* III 167).
[46] *JP* VI 6491 (X² A 15).

3

Kierkegaard's View of Man and Woman

In our age, when practically everything is opened to debate, the most recent years have seen the question of woman's position in society come especially to the fore. However, this question cannot be answered satisfactorily unless at the same time man's position is continually taken into account. In this way the debate actually focuses on the relation between man and woman, a subject to which—perhaps to the surprise of many—Kierkegaard devoted considerable attention. In my opinion, Kierkegaard will be able to bring to the current debate new and original points of view that no doubt will be regarded today as very controversial but in the long run will just as surely manifest their validity and justification. As one of the most profound psychologists and as a keen observer of people and their relation to each other, Kierkegaard had a well-founded and consistently thought-out view on this question. For this reason, whether one agrees or disagrees with him, he is worth listening to when this subject is up for debate.

As a slight matter of curiosity in connection with our subject, it may be stated that Kierkegaard's first publication was a little article on the emancipation of woman in *Kjøbenhavns flyvende Post* in 1834.[1] It was written in his ironic period of early youth and was

---

[1] *SV* XIII, p. 4.

prompted by P. E. Lind's satire entitled "In Defense of the Higher Origin of Woman." Kierkegaard's contribution is entitled "Another Defense of Woman's High Aptitude" and is an amusing and naïve ironizing on the emanicipation of women. He foresees, among other things, that when women begin to appear as critics in the spheres of art and scholarship there will no "longer be mention of Kantians, Hegelians, etc.; no, in the future these names will be replaced by *The Blues, The Reds*, etc."[2]

Taken as a whole, it is noteworthy that approximately a third of Kierkegaard's authorship deals in some form or another with the relation between man and woman. This demonstrates something of the crucial importance he attached to this question.

In order to understand Kierkegaard's views, we must clearly understand that the basis for his view of man and woman is his conception of the human being as a synthesis of two contrasting components—namely, the temporal and the eternal—of which the eternal or the spiritual as the actuating principle is the more important. This conception builds primarily upon the Christian view of the human being as consisting of body, soul, and spirit, and by stressing the decisive importance of the spiritual this conception is fundamentally anti-materialistic. Thus it becomes every person's task to unite these opposites in the right way in order thereby to fulfil one's destiny—namely, to become an independent personality, a self. This can occur only through many levels of development, of which the most important are the esthetic, the ethical, and the religious.

A human being begins existence as an individual, which means that one is totally dependent upon one's inherited nature and the race. On this lowest level, the race—that is, the hereditary characteristics and the milieu—is dominant, and the individual [*Individet*] has to work its own way step by step and champion its own distinctive character. On this level there is no essential difference between man and woman, because the most important task for both is to be of service to the race in terms of maintaining and reproducing it. Kierkegaard compares this relation to a plant in which the male and the female flower are on the same stem.[3] As far as the erotic relation is concerned, it is the race, understood as the species, that directs the relation between the sexes. Of this, one of Kierkegaard's many

---

[2] *SV* XIII, p. 8.
[3] *Either/Or*, I, p. 76 (*SV* I 59); cf. *SV* XIII, p. 75 fn. [*From the Papers of One Still Living*].

pseudonyms says that when two people "in union and in erotic love form a self," they are in actuality deceived, "for in the very same moment nature triumphs over the individuals; nature is victorious, while the individuals are reduced to being in its service." Thus the deceit is due to the belief of the man and the woman that it is love [*Kærligheden*] that has brought them together, and then it turns out that the driving force was the sexual instinct and that the real goal was the propagation of the race.[4]

A big and decisive step forward takes place when the individual progresses so far that the psychic nature can balance the physical or sensate[5] nature, as it is also called, in this way creating a harmony or a synthesis between these two elements. Historically, this development attained its full scope in ancient Greece. There the ideal—and this was true for both man and woman—was the beautiful individuality. The goal of the synthesis was to create the beautiful, and beauty is the "unity of the psychic and the somatic."[6] Consequently, beauty was the common ideal, and yet there was already here an intimation of a specific difference between the masculine and the feminine. One of Kierkegaard's pseudonyms says of this:

> It is true that Greek beauty conceives of man and of woman in the same way, as nonspiritual. Nevertheless there is a distinction within this likeness. The spiritual has its expression in the face. In the beauty of the man, the face and its expression are more essential than in the beauty of the woman, although the eternal youthfulness of plastic art constantly prevents the more deeply spiritual from appearing.

He says further: "Venus arises from the sea and is represented in a position of repose, a position that reduces the expression of the face to the nonessential. If, on the other hand, Apollo is to be represented, it would no more be appropriate to have him sleep than it would be to have Jupiter do so. Apollo would thereby become ugly and Jupiter ridiculous."[7]

---

[4] *Stages on Life's Way* (New York: Schocken, 1967), p. 56 (*SV* VI 45). This view is dominant in Arthur Schopenhauer, *Metaphysik der Geschlechtsliebe* [The Metaphysics of the Love of the Sexes].

[5] In Kierkegaard and the pseudonymous writers, this word does not have overtones of the sexual but denotes a greater dependence on the physiological. See *The Concept of Anxiety*, pp. 64-65 (*SV* IV 334).

[6] Ibid., p. 69 (*SV* IV 339).

[7] Ibid., p. 65 (*SV* IV 335).

This principle of beauty was broken by Socrates who, according to tradition, was the ugliest man in Greece, or, as Kierkegaard says: "He was, yes, he was the homeliest man in the whole town, the homeliest man among the most beautiful people."[8] With Socrates, the spiritual principle emerges; this means that in the human being there begins a longing for the infinite—that is, for something that lies beyond the limited visible world. The idea of beauty signifies harmony within the finite, the terrestrial world; the principle of infinity signifies that it now becomes the human being's task to form a new synthesis—namely, a synthesis between the physical and the psychical on the one side and spirit on the other. Here we arrive at a very crucial point—namely, that in this longing for something beyond, this longing directed toward infinity, the salient feature of masculinity emerges. Hitherto there had been no essential difference between masculinity and femininity, as we saw in the Greek mentality where, as it is said, "Everyone was only a beautiful individuality, but femininity was not surmised"[9]—in other words, the idea of masculinity did not exist either. As Socrates introduces the masculine principle in his pointing to the infinite, the feminine principle also gets its placement. The kingdom of woman becomes the kingdom of beauty; the man's becomes the possibilities and the problems of the infinite. This can be briefly expressed as follows: "Woman is substance, man is reflection."[10] Woman has a closer relationship to nature, while the man's domain is thought and the abstract.

For the most part, however, it is Christianity that has deepened and spiritualized the positions of man and woman and established their relation to each other on a higher plane. According to Kierkegaard, Christianity has pointed out the equality of all human beings before God, because God has placed a longing for the eternal in every human being. To possess this eternal constitutent is the essential in being human; therefore this possession makes all human beings essentially equal. But at the same time Christianity points out that when it is a question of carrying out earthly tasks there are differences. This view of being human was Kierkegaard's point of departure from the very beginning of the authorship, and it is also this view upon which Kierkegaard's pseudonym Judge William builds when in the second

---

[8] *Works of Love*, p. 341 (*SV* IX 351).
[9] *Either/Or*, I, p. 87 (ed. tr.) (*SV* I 70).
[10] Ibid., p. 426 (ed. tr.) (*SV* I 398).

part of *Either/Or* he discusses the question of marriage and the relation between man and woman.

Judge William powerfully and convincingly champions the significance of marriage and points out the different tasks that are assigned to man and woman respectively. He maintains the distinction that woman's essential interest lies within finitude, while man's element is restlessness and a longing that goes beyond the boundaries of finitude. It must, however, be said that what is propounded here is an ideal, but an ideal that has an abode in actuality. The idea Judge William and Kierkegaard employ—that the eternal is a genuine and essential presupposition for human life—would, of course, be rejected on the basis of a materialistic point of view, but as a consequence the materialist retrogresses to the more primitive forms in human development whereby sexual differences are again levelled, as is apparent in many instances today.

The following thesis constitutes a point of departure for Judge William's description of the relation between man and woman: "The woman explains finitude, the man is hunting for infinitude." Precisely because the woman explains finitude—that is, earthly existence— and feels at home in it, Judge William eulogizes her as follows:

> A woman comprehends finitude, she understands it from the bottom up; that is why she is lovely, as every woman essentially is; that is why she is sweet and charming, as no man ever is; that is why she is happy as no man can or ought to be; that is why she is in harmony with existence as no man can or ought to be. Thus it can be said that her life is happier than man's, for finitude can certainly make a person happy; infinitude *per se* never can. She is more perfect than man, for surely the one who explains something is more perfect than the one who is hunting for an explanation.[11]

Judge William also describes what a solace it was for man when woman was created.

> When man was created, he stood there as nature's lord and prince, nature's magnificence and splendor; all the riches of finitude merely awaited his nod, but he did not comprehend what he should do with it all. He looked at it, but everything seemed to vanish in this mental gaze; it seemed to him that if he moved he would bypass it all in one single step. Thus he stood, an imposing figure, lost in thought and yet comic, for one had to smile at this rich man who did not know how to use his riches, but

---

[11] Ibid., II, p. 316 (ed. tr.) (*SV* II 279).

also tragic, for he could not use them. Then the woman was created. She was in no quandary; she knew at once what to do, was ready to begin immediately without any fuss, without any preparation.[12]

Judge William goes on to elucidate this difference between woman and man which, seen most profoundly, is due to the woman's having her primary task within finitude while the latter with his longing goes beyond it.

> This is the way it has to be, and each one has one's own pain. The woman bears children in pain, but the man conceives ideas in pain; the woman is not supposed to know the anxiety of doubt or the agony of despair, she is not supposed to stand outside the idea, but she has it second hand. Because woman explains life in this way, she is man's deepest life, but a life that is supposed to be hidden and secret, as the life of the root always is.[13]

Here we see that Judge William, after having first stressed woman's advantage and in a certain sense calling her more perfect than man, now speaks of man's spiritual superiority. "The anxiety of doubt and the agony of despair" are precisely the conditions human beings get into when the synthesis is not only to be made between the physical and the psychical, but between the physical and the psychical on the one side and the spiritual on the other. Woman is spared these pangs because the synthesis she forms is primarily physical-psychical and consequently resides within the idea of harmony and beauty. The fact that the spiritual element plays a more essential role for man means that he is exposed to more drastic psychical and spiritual struggles and an internal split. As a consequence man becomes the leader in this sphere, for he fights through the contradictions and conflicts of existence in a more reflective and conscious manner. But this is not saying that the woman is supposed "to stand outside the idea, but she has it second hand."[14]

Another consequence of this is that the idea of the emancipation of women, which began to be a live issue in Kierkegaard's day, is very sharply rejected by Judge William. With his romantic attitude toward love and marriage, he cannot reconcile himself to the idea that woman, in addition to being woman, also wants to act the man.

---

[12] Ibid., p. 315 (ed. tr.) (*SV* II 278).
[13] Ibid., p. 316 (ed. tr.) (*SV* II 279).
[14] Ibid.

But [he says] it does not happen, it shall not and cannot happen, so let the evil spirits try it; the stupid people who have no concept of what it is to be a man, neither of the greatness or the contemptibleness of it, have no idea of woman's perfection in her imperfection! Could there really be one single woman simple and vain and pitiable enough to believe that under the category of man she could become more perfect than man, not to perceive that her loss would be irreparable? No black-hearted seducer could think up a more dangerous dogma than this, for once he has deluded her into thinking this, he has her completely in his power, abandoned to his will; she can be nothing for the man but a prey to his whims, while as a woman she can be everything for him.

Judge William's belief that the emancipation of women is a dangerous movement for woman is prompted by the consideration that if woman makes herself equal with man—for example, in the domain of the erotic—he will have no special obligation to her; she will be completely at his disposal, and, as the weaker one in the erotic and sexual sense, she will be the one who loses most. Judge William goes on to say: "But the poor fellows do not know what they are doing, they themselves are not much good at being men, and instead of learning how to be men they want to corrupt women and be united with them on the condition that they themselves remain what they are, half-men, and women advance to the same wretchedness."[15]

He also relates that he once heard a proposal that man and woman should dress alike. If one dared even for a moment to imagine "this enormity," Judge William believes that one would immediately miss beauty in a woman and thus understand what it means to her.

As is evident from these statements on the emancipation of women, Judge William believes that in opposing it he is actually defending woman. In other words, he believes that woman, just as she is, is indispensable to man, and he declares, "Let man give up his claim to be nature's lord and prince, let him yield that place to woman; she is nature's mistress, it understands her and she understands it, it is at her beck and call. The reason that she is everything to man is that she presents him with finitude; without her he is unstable, unhappy, cannot find rest, has no abode."[16]

That woman is man's firm fulcrum in existence is also evident in Judge William's comment "that Scripture does not say that a woman

---

[15] Ibid., p. 317 (ed. tr.) (*SV* II 279-80).
[16] Ibid., p. 318 (ed. tr.) (*SV* II 280-81).

should leave father and mother and cling to her husband, as one might think it would say, for after all, woman is the weaker one who seeks light from the man. No, it says that the man should leave father and mother and cling to his wife, for to the extent that she bestows finitude on him, she is stronger than he."[17]

Judge William also touches on the difference in the way a man and a woman prays. Of woman he says:

> ...for it is a woman's nature to pray for others. Imagine her in whatever station of life you please, any age whatsoever, imagine her praying, and as a rule you will find her praying for others, for her parents, for her beloved, for her husband, for her children, always for others. Man by nature prays for himself. He has his specific task, his specific place. Thus his resignation is different; even in prayer he is militant.[18]

Judge William likewise says that there is a difference with regard to faith, declaring that in a certain sense a woman has more faith than a man,

> for the woman believes that for God all things are possible; the man believes that for God some things are impossible. The woman becomes more and more fervent in her humble petitioning. The man gives up more and more, until he finds the immovable point from which he cannot be ousted. This is because man by nature doubts, and therefore all his wisdom bears the mark of this.[19]

Judge William's highest praise, however, goes to woman as mother. He says as follows: "A woman's life as mother is an actuality so infinitely rich in variation that my love has enough to do discovering something new each day. As mother the woman is never in a situation where one is compelled to say that in this situation she is her most beautiful; as mother she is constantly in this situation, and mother love is as soft as pure gold and pliant in every decision, and yet whole." And further: "To what a variety of collisions mother love is exposed, and how beautiful the mother is every time her self-renouncing, self-sacrificing love comes out victoriously."[20] Or "As a bride woman is more beautiful than as a maiden, as a mother she is

---

[17] Ibid. (ed. tr.) (*SV* II 281).
[18] Ibid., pp. 319-20 (ed. tr.) (*SV* II 282).
[19] Ibid., p. 320 (ed. tr.) (*SV* II 283).
[20] *Stages*, p. 137 (ed. tr.) (*SV* VI 130).

more beautiful than as a bride, as a wife and mother she is a good word in season, and with the years she becomes more beautiful."[21]

Accenting woman's important task as mother goes together with Judge William's view of the meaning of marriage, which he defends against any and all denunciations. It is of interest that when Kierkegaard writes later in one of his journals that he "has written one of the most inspired defenses of marriage,"[22] he is thinking specifically of Judge William's description. For William, marriage is the focal undertaking in existence, and he gives a very ideal but also very comprehensive picture of it. For a marriage to be able to be described as in harmony with its idea, two qualifications must be present: it must be entered into on the basis of love [*Kjærlighed*], and for both parties it must contain an unconditional commitment before something higher, be it society or God. According to Judge William's romantic conception, erotic love [*Elskov*] or love [*Kjærlighed*] already contains an element of something eternal; this element becomes deepened and strengthened by the ethical commitment one makes upon entering into marriage. As to the resolution that precedes it, Judge William believes that it involves something different for the man and for the woman. A man's way to resolution proceeds through many reflections, while a woman surmises in a flash the problems that may arise, but her faith in love [*Kjærlighed*] makes it possible for her to make the leap to the religious resolution that ought to be a presupposition for the wedding.

Judge William does not believe that a marriage ought to be entered into on the basis of finite and prosaic considerations and calculations, and in a not merely detailed but also very amusing way he refutes three of the most important arguments advanced for getting married. There are some, for example, who believe that one should get married in order "to improve and refine one's character," or "in order to have children," or "in order to have a home."[23] He continues in this vein: "I have mentioned only three, because they uniformly seem to have an integrity of their own, because they do respond to some single factor in marriage, although in their bias they become just as ridiculous as they are unesthetic and irreligious. I

---

[21] Ibid., p. 141 (ed. tr.) (*SV* VI 135).

[22] *Papirer* X⁶ B 115. Cf. *JP* VI 6882 (XI¹ A 210): ". . . who has described marriage and all these aspects of human existence more beautifully, more charmingly, than I?"

[23] *Either/Or*, II, pp. 65-78 (*SV* II 59-70).

made no mention of a multitude of altogether contemptible motives, because they are not even laughable."[24]

As the primary condition for a marriage lived according to his idea, Judge William adduces:

> frankness, honesty, publicity on the largest scale possible, for this is the life-principle of love, and secrecy here is its death. But this is not as easily done as said, and it truly takes courage to carry it out consistently . . . . It takes courage to be willing to show oneself as one really is, it takes courage not to want to buy oneself immunity from a little humiliation if one can do this by a certain secretiveness, and not to want to buy a little more stature when one can do it by being reserved and reticent. It takes courage to will to be sound and healthy, honestly and uprightly to will the true.[25]

Finally, it must be mentioned that Judge William attempts to repudiate all the unjustified attacks upon woman and upon marriage launched by the esthetes in the well-known section of *Stages on Life's Way* entitled "*In vino veritas*," in which they try to diminish woman's positive meaning by irony at her expense. One of these esthetes maintains that woman can never be taken seriously, that she "is properly construed only under the category of jest."[26] He says of woman that she "has a pristine privilege to be changed in less than twenty-four hours into the most innocent and forgivable galimathias, because far be it from her honest soul to want to deceive anyone—she meant everything she said—now she is saying the opposite, but with the same lovable sincerity, for now she will die for the opposite."[27]

A second esthete believes that woman can have only a negative meaning for man. He declares:

> Many a man became a genius because of a girl, many a man became a hero because of a girl, many a man became a poet because of a girl, many a man became a saint because of a girl—but he did not become a genius because of the girl he got, for with her he would have become just a cabinet official; he did not become a hero because of the girl he got, for because of her he would have become just a general; he did not become a poet because of the girl he got, for because of her he would have become just a father; he did not become a saint because of the girl he got, for he got none at all and wanted none but the one and only, just

---

[24] Ibid., p. 89 (ed. tr.) (*SV* II 80).
[25] Ibid., p. 106 (ed. tr.) (*SV* II 96).
[26] *Stages*, p. 61 (ed. tr.) (*SV* VI 49).
[27] Ibid., p. 62 (ed. tr.) (*SV* VI 50).

as each of the others became a genius, a hero, a poet with the aid of the girl he did not get.[28]

A third esthete sees his life task to be fathoming the mystery of woman, and believes he can do this best as a fashion designer. He declares, "If one wishes to get to know women, one hour in my boutique is worth more than ages on the outside;"[29] and he maintains that "fashion, after all, is the one and only thing she is always thinking about, the only thing she is able to think about together, with, and in the midst of everything else."[30]

Yet another esthete, named Johannes the Seducer, looks at woman solely from the point of view of pleasure; like all seducers, he wants to have the fun but does not wish to be bound. As he himself says, these devotees of erotic love "continually eat only the bait— they are never trapped."[31]

The various speeches in "*In vino veritas*" contain many interesting psychological observations on woman. But because of their one-sidedness and because of their disregard for the positive aspects, they end as a caricature of her, or as Kierkegaard himself expresses it later, they "illuminate women essentially but nevertheless falsely."[32]

Judge William, too, repudiates all these assertions about the nature of woman as one-sided, because they look at woman only from an esthetic point of view and, moreover, exclusively emphasize the negative. He considers it wrong to look at woman isolated from marriage and from man and maintains that "precisely because marriage is the center, woman must be viewed in relation to it, and the same goes for the man, and all this talk about and viewing of each sex separately is confused and profane, for what God has joined together, what life has destined for each other, ought also to be thought together."[33]

Judge William is the pseudonym Kierkegaard used most to illuminate marriage and the relation between man and woman in general. But the question then comes up as to whether Judge William's views coincide with Kierkegaard's own views. In the main this can be

---

[28] Ibid., p. 70 (ed. tr.) (*SV* VI 59-60).
[29] Ibid., p. 76 (ed. tr.) (*SV* VI 66).
[30] Ibid., p. 77 (ed. tr.) (*SV* VI 68-69).
[31] Ibid., p. 84 (ed. tr.) (*SV* VI 74).
[32] *JP* V 5755 (V A 110).
[33] *Stages*, p. 144 (ed. tr.) (*SV* VI 138-39).

answered in the affirmative, and it can be shown that in his own signed upbuilding literature Kierkegaard expresses essentially the same attitude as Judge William in these areas, even though Judge William's thoughts are rather romantic, while Kierkegaard's are less complex and rhapsodic.

In *Works of Love*, which is Kierkegaard's major ethical writing, there is also some discussion of the emancipation of women. He first of all points out that Christianity once and for all made clear that before God there is an essential equality among all human beings, "but the distinctions of earthly existence it has not taken away."[34] Of the immense change that occurs in the relation between man and woman with Christianity, Kierkegaard says:

> What abominations has the world not seen in the relation between man and woman—that she, almost like an animal, was a despised creature compared to the male, a creature of another species! What battles there have been to establish women on equal terms with men in the secular world! But Christianity makes only the transformation of infinity and does it, therefore, in all stillness. Outwardly in a way the old remains—for the man shall be the woman's master and she shall be submissive to him, but in inwardness everything is transformed, transformed with the aid of this little question to the woman, whether she has deliberated with her conscience about having this man—for a master, for otherwise she does not get him. Yet the question of conscience about a matter of conscience makes her in inwardness before God absolutely equal with the man.[35]

But it would again be a misunderstanding of Christianity to think that it wants to abolish the relative, earthly distinctions between man and woman. For this reason the idea of the emancipation of women, seen from the Christian point of view, is wrong. Kierkegaard writes of this:

> Foolish people have foolishly busied themselves in the name of Christianity to make it obvious in the world that women have equal rights with men—Christianity has never demanded or desired this. It has done everything for woman if she Christianly will be satisfied with what is Christian. If she will not, for her loss she gains only a mediocre compensation in the little fragmentary externals she can win by worldly threats.[36]

---

[34] *Works of Love*, p. 81 (*SV* IX 71).
[35] Ibid., p. 139 (*SV* IX 133).
[36] Ibid., p. 139-40 (*SV* IX 133-34).

Kierkegaard states another reason for his not being able to endorse the emancipation of women. It is found in a journal entry and is linked to his assessing the mounting confusion of the age:

There is really something to it that in the last resort women are a bit more self-sacrificing. It is probably because they live more quietly and withdrawn and thus a bit closer to ideality. They are not as likely to acquire the market-price standard the way a man does, who from the outset is on the go in life. The saving factor for women (which is why one still sees in them the traces and expressions of individuality, the boldness to grasp a single thought and to dare hold on to it) is the distance from life which is granted her for a period. The quieter life sometimes has the result that she becomes somewhat more herself than does a man, who already even as a lad is demoralized by having to be like the others, and as a youth, to say nothing of the adult, is completely demoralized by learning how things go in practical life, in actuality. This very knowledge is the ruination of him. If girls were brought up in the same way—then good night to the whole human race. And no doubt the emancipation of women, which tends toward this kind of upbringing, is the invention of the devil.[37]

In one of his upbuilding discourses, Kierkegaard stresses in particular woman's "humble faith with respect to the extraordinary" and her capacity to concentrate on the individual tasks in contrast to man's fragmentation, which is related to his having an excess of reflection. He speaks especially of her sorrow over sin, but this also has other applications:

Compared to woman, man does seem to have many thoughts (it is a question, especially in this respect, whether this is a distinct advantage, since in addition he also has so many half-thoughts), and man does seem to be stronger than the weak one, woman, has many more ways out, knows far better how to manage. But then, again, woman has one thing, one thing—indeed, the very thing that is her element: one. One wish, not many wishes—no, just one wish, but then, too, the soul is totally involved in it; one thought, not many thoughts—no, just one thought, but by the power of her passion an enormous power; one sorrow, not many sorrows—no, one sorrow, but so deep in her heart that one sorrow is certainly much more than many sorrows; one sorrow—yes, just one sorrow, but then, too, it is the deepest one—sorrow over her sin, as this woman who was a sinner.

---

[37] *JP* IV 4992 (X¹ A 459).

Kierkegaard goes on to say: "When it comes to thinking, let man have more earnestness; when it comes to feelings, passion, decision, when it is a matter of not frustrating decision by thoughts, intentions, resolutions, when it is a matter of not defeating oneself by getting very close to a decision without, however, making a decision—here the woman has more earnestness . . . ."[38]

Kierkegaard maintains, as does Judge William, that woman's essential task must be in the home, domesticity, the upbringing of the coming generation. She is also the one who can create silence in the home—that is, an atmosphere of peace and quiet so that whatever is worthwhile and essential in life is not drowned out in the noise and hubbub of the age "over even the most insignificant undertaking." That is, according to Kierkegaard, everything in our age

> is intended only to amuse the senses or to stir up the mass, the multitude, the public—stir up hubbub.
>
> And man, sharp wit that he is, doesn't sleep in order that he may invent new, ever new means of increasing noise, of circulating uproar and triviality with the greatest possible haste and on the greatest possible scale. Everything is soon turned upside down. As far as significance is concerned, communication has soon reached its lowest point and at the same time as far as speedy and overflowing propagation is concerned, communicators have just about reached their highest point. For what is got out in such hot haste, and,—on the other hand, what has a greater circulation than—gossip! Bring about silence!
>
> Women can do this. Quite an extraordinary superiority is required if a man is to command the silence of men by his presence. On the other hand, every woman can command it in her own domain, her own circle, if she—not selfishly, but humbly serving one higher—wills it.
>
> But nature has really not been partial to women, nor has Christianity either. As it is, it is human, and thus also feminine, modestly to want to have a significance in one's own sphere, to want to be, yes, a power. Then, too, a woman can exercise power in many different ways—by her beauty, by her charm, by her gifts, by her daring power of imagination, by her happy disposition. She can also seek to become a power in a noisy way. The latter is ugly and false, the former weak and uncertain. But if you want to be a power, woman, let me confide in you how—learn silence! Learn silence by yourself![39]

---

[38] *SV* XII 250 ["The Woman Who Was a Sinner"] (ed. tr.).

[39] *For Self-Examination* (Minneapolis: Augsburg, 1940), pp. 57-58 (*SV* XII 334-35).

By silence Kierkegaard means primarily that woman must be personally sensitive to whatever has eternal worth so that she can create in her home a basic mood of peacefulness and sensitivity in contrast to the world's restlessness and busyness.

But in order for woman to be able to create this silence, she must possess a quality that Kierkegaard rates highest in woman, namely, "domesticity," by which he means that she must know how to manage her work and time in her home so that it also becomes a place for whatever has spiritual value. This quality has equal value whether it is found in a woman in the most modest humble circumstances or in a queen. Kierkegaard expresses it this way:

> Take a simple, middle-class woman; if she can truthfully be said to be domestic—honor be to her! I bow as deeply before her as before a queen. On the other hand, if the queen does not have this quality, she is only a mediocre woman. Take a young girl who can hardly be called a beauty; if she possesses this quality (and a young girl can)—honor be to her! On the other hand, take a radiant beauty and, for the sake of comparison, give her all sorts of talents to boot and, for the sake of comparison, let her be renowned. But if she does not have this art, indeed, has never had respect for it, this beauty, with all her talents, charm, and renown, is still a mediocre woman.[40]

In the following more theoretical account of Kierkegaard's view of man and woman, we will see how Kierkegaard deals with this question partly from a psychological and partly from an ethical-religious point of view. As a psychologist, Kierkegaard knew how to identify with other people's innermost feelings and thoughts, to enter vitally into their secret conflicts and psychic needs, and to reproduce their experiences in imaginative form. An excellent example of this is his pseudonymous portrayal of the three familiar tragic literary characters: Marie Beaumarchais, Donna Elvira, and Margaret in *Faust*, all of whom were betrayed by their lovers. With great sympathetic insight, these "silhouettes"[41] show what an enormous tragedy it is for a woman to be deceived by the one to whom she has given her love [*Kjærlighed*]. She thereby loses not only her beloved and the meaning of her existence, but also her faith in love, and must constantly be plagued by doubt as to whether she had been loved at all. The three women discussed here keep brooding on these thoughts

---

[40] Ibid., pp. 59-60 (*SV* XII 336).
[41] *Either/Or*, I, pp. 163ff. (ed. tr.) (*SV* I 143ff.).

and thus are prevented from coming to the religious level of life by means of a resolution of their problem through repentance.

In *The Seducer's Diary*, there is another portrayal of a woman who is made unhappy by becoming the object of a subtle and sophisticated seduction in which the seducer methodically and with cold calculation carries out his designs on the innocent girl. The portrayal contains many acute psychological insights, which Kierkegaard himself thought could serve "as a preliminary study for a very serious and not merely superficial research"[42] pertaining to the relation between man and woman.

On the basis of his own unhappy broken engagement, Kierkegaard, writing pseudonymously, has also described very concretely and fully the deep conflicts that can arise in a relationship of love between a man and a woman. There is a precise description of the psychological characteristics of the two characters: a reflective and intrinsically self-inclosed [*indesluttet*] young man and a cheerful, spontaneous, naïve young girl. The course of the conflict is described in the journal almost from day to day, and in conclusion there is an explanation of the deeper causes of the conflict and an explanation as to why the relationship had to end unhappily. The pseudonym, Vigilius Haufniensis, who in the book *The Concept of Anxiety* compares the psychical aspects of man and woman, maintains that one essential difference is that woman has more anxiety than man. For Kierkegaard, the presence of anxiety in human beings is a testimony that human beings, seen most profoundly, feel insecure in their earthly existence because they unconsciously apprehend that it also has an eternal destiny. Therefore, if woman is described as having more anxiety than man, it must not be understood as an imperfection in her, since it is expressly said that "the greatness of anxiety is a prophecy of the greatness of the perfection."[43]

With regard to this greater anxiety in woman, Kierkegaard notes in his journals that it makes her an easier prey for the seducer. He says: "The Seducer's secret is simply that he knows that woman is anxiety."[44]

That woman has more anxiety than man is related to her being more dependent on her physical constitution. Her essential task consists in bringing harmony into the relation between the physical

---

[42] *JP* V 5730 (V B 53:26).
[43] *The Concept of Anxiety*, p. 64 (*SV* IV 334).
[44] *JP* V 5730 (V B 53:26).

nature and the psychical nature, just as her life also culminates in motherhood. Thus in woman the psychical is dominant, while in man it ought to be the intellectual.

The dominance of the psychical in woman expresses itself in her having more feeling, more imagination than man. She is influenced more by sympathy and antipathy, and this again says that personal contacts mean more to her than the abstract and intellectual environment in which man has a greater interest. Woman is more thoughtful of others,[45] while man is more self-assertive. These differences are later summarized by another pseudonym as follows: "However much more tender and sensitive woman may be than man, she has neither the egotistical concept of the self nor, in a decisive sense, intellectuality. But the feminine nature is devotedness, givingness, and it is unfeminine if it is not." But in order that woman may not be misused because of this devotedness, which is called a divine gift and treasure, "nature has affectionately equipped her with an instinct so sensitive that by comparison the most superior masculine reflection is as nothing." It says further: ". . . blindfolded, she instinctively sees more clearly than the most clear-sighted reflection; instinctively she sees what she should admire, that to which she should give herself."[46]

It is woman's nature to give herself totally, and only then is she happy. Man's devotedness, his giving of himself, will never be complete, because he constantly remains conscious of his giving of himself; he does not lose himself in it as does woman. Here, therefore, is the greatest possibility to misuse woman's love if man does not see his responsibility and his duty. But through the relationship to a higher power, through the relationship to God, both parties can come to a freedom in their unfreedom and emotional dependence on each other. Only through the relationship to God can each become a self and thereby also become equal. This is expressed by one of Kierkegaard's pseudonyms as follows: "In the relationship to God, where the distinction man-woman vanishes, it holds for men as well as for women that devotion is the self, and that in the giving of oneself the self is gained. This holds equally for man and woman, although probably in most cases the woman actually relates to God

---

[45] Compare with Judge William's comment that woman "is far better qualified to pray for others than is man." *Either/Or*, II, p. 320 (ed. tr.) (*SV* II 282).

[46] *The Sickness unto Death*, pp. 49-50 fn. (*SV* XI 162 fn.).

only through the man.''[47] The statement that woman "probably in most cases" relates to God through the man is consistent with Kierkegaard's thinking that man fights through the religious conflicts more consciously and decisively, whereby he often can be instructive to woman in these specific areas. However, woman as an independent being ultimately has to decide for herself how she is going to relate to the deepest religious questions. For this reason Kierkegaard constantly points out that despite all the differences, especially with regard to devotedness, a woman, seen from a religious point of view, is essentially equal to man. He says of this: "Of course every religious view, like every more profound philosophical view, sees women . . . as essentially identical with man; but it is not foolish enough to forget for that reason the truth of the difference, esthetically and ethically understood.''[48]

In the ethical sphere, then, Kierkegaard believes there is a demonstrable difference between man and woman. Woman, for example, attaches more importance to observing the accepted norms and conventions of society. Woman's ethical stance can be designated as a "sense of shame" or "modesty," by which Kierkegaard understands woman's solicitude for her reputation, her taking into consideration what others think and accept. He plainly states: ". . . in a woman the sense of shame is strongest, stronger than life; she would rather relinquish her life than relinquish her modesty.''[49] In modesty, she respects the eternal world order, which for her is an expression of the true ethics. A similar attitude is found in ancient Greece, where it also was the sense of shame that "forcefully yet mysteriously binds the individual to the reins of the state.''[50] Not until Socrates do we find a personal ethics signifying that the individual acts out of an inner ethical conviction of what is right. This becomes man's ethical ideal especially and means, as already stated, that while woman remains within the harmony, man throws himself into the attempt to reorganize his existence, which in the first round leads to schism and inner conflict. It is actually here that Kierkegaard sees the important difference between man and woman; it is found within the sphere that Kierkegaard regards as the most important in human life—namely, the ethical-religious sphere. According to

---

[47] Ibid., p. 50 fn. (*SV* XI 163); cf. *JP* V 5007 (XI² A 192).
[48] *JP* IV 4989 (V B 53:25).
[49] *SV* XI 274 ["The Woman Who Was a Sinner"] (ed. tr.).
[50] *The Concept of Irony*, p. 190 (ed. tr.) (*SV* XIII 247).

Kierkegaard, the masses do not get beyond the esthetic stage;[51] some do reach the ethical stage, but only very few reach the religious stage.

Man's battle with himself and his attempt to form a synthesis on a higher level Kierkegaard calls "redoubling" [*Fordoblelse*]. Redoubling manifests, as one of the pseudonyms declares, "contradiction in passions," that is, being able to hold on to two passions simultaneously. For example, one abandons on the one hand the thought that a specific wish can be fulfilled and simultaneously *believes* in the possibility of the fulfillment. Here we encounter the category of the absurd. A conflict such as this would disrupt the feminine psyche, and Kierkegaard believes that only man has the "toughness"[52] to be able to keep this tension in his existence. One of the pseudonyms says of this conflict: "A woman can have passion as strong as or perhaps stronger than a man, but contradiction in passion is not her task, such as the task of simultaneously giving up and retaining the wish."[53] He goes on to say: "A woman cannot involve herself in double illumination and double reflection; her reflection is only single. If she wants to give up the wish, then reflection is the conflict between the life of the wish and the death of the resignation, but to will both at the same time is for her impossible—indeed, perhaps even impossible to understand."[54] In a journal entry, Kierkegaard puts it even more strongly, declaring that "no woman can bear [redoubling]; she will lose her mind if she is to be put under the tension of this strenuousness."[55]

Kierkegaard steadfastly maintains that with regard to redoubling man and woman are different, and even if Christianity has made them equal, this difference continues to exist. He says, for example: "To say that Christianity makes man and woman equal, and therefore the woman must relate to Christianity the same way as the man, is baseless talk. Christianity does indeed make man and woman equal, but it still does not change their natural qualifications . . . ." And he further insists that "on the level of the immediate and direct, women certainly have superiority both in delicacy and in depth and inward-

---

[51] *The Point of View*, p. 82 (ed. tr.) (*SV* XIII 567), where Kierkegaard declares that the majority of human beings "merely live out their lives within the psychic-somatic factors of the synthesis," which means that they remain within the esthetic sphere.

[52] *JP* IV 5007 (XI² A 192).

[53] *Stages*, p. 280 (ed. tr.) (*SV* VI 282).

[54] Ibid., p. 281 (ed. tr.) (*SV* VI 283).

[55] *JP* IV 5007 (XI² A 192).

ness, but as soon as there is a dialectic,'' woman has difficulties.[56] Therefore it is characteristic for woman to reach the religious stage from the esthetic stage by a leap, consequently without involving herself in the personal ethics into which the man ventures. We encounter this thought already in Judge William when he declares: "In her immediacy, woman is primarily esthetic, but precisely because she is that way primarily, the transition into the religious is also *ex tempore*."[57] That woman is primarily esthetic is due to the fact that the centre of gravity in her life is within the esthetic, earthly existence, which at any time can be smashed to pieces for the individual. If this happens to woman, she does not, according to Judge William, have the personal ethics a man has to hold on to, but may turn directly to the religious.

To avoid misunderstanding, however, it must be noted that within the esthetic sphere there are also specific decorous and moral norms that people respect out of modesty, a sense of propriety toward each other. Thus when woman makes the leap from the esthetic into the religious, she also leaves out a specific form of the ethical, the primary aim of which is practical and earthly. By her transition to the religious, the modesty she hitherto has had with respect to the universal external laws becomes a "*holy* modesty," thus a modesty before God.

If there is a difference between a woman's and a man's transition to the religious, it is, looked at most profoundly, connected with man's craving reaching beyond this existence—regarded as a harmonious cosmos—while woman seeks content in life by unfolding her natural talents and aptitudes. Karen Blixen expresses a similar view in *En Baaltale*, where she says: "Man's center of gravity, the substance of his being, is in what he does and achieves in life; woman's is in what she is."[58] Thus woman's being contains in advance what shapes her life; she already *is* what is to be unfolded. Man first has to win his worth, and this is especially true in the spiritual domain. This could also be epitomized as follows: woman represents actuality, while man aspires after possibility. Woman is humble; she more readily perceives what is impossible, lies beyond her energies, and accedes. Man, however, is proud; he first has to test the impossible in order thereby, if possible, to realize his weakness.

---

[56] *JP* IV 5008 (XI[2] A 193).

[57] *Stages*, p. 163 (ed. tr.) (*SV* VI 158).

[58] Karen Blixen, *En Baaltale* (Copenhagen: Berlingske Forlag, 1953), p. 18.

But in man's high striving woman can be a beneficial corrective for him. On this point, Kierkegaard says:

> On the whole, the woman is and ought to be a corrective in proclaiming the ethical-religious. One must not make it rigorous for men and have another kind for women, but in making it rigorous one ought to respect woman as an authority also and temper it through assistance from that source. And for the sake of the cause, a woman perhaps may lift the burden just as well as a man precisely because she has fewer ideas, and also fewer half-ideas, than the man, and thus more feeling, imagination, and passion.[59]

It is also interesting that in another journal entry Kierkegaard advances the unity of the feminine and the masculine elements as the highest ideal in the religious sphere: "In a certain sense woman is by nature better suited for essentially religious service, for it is a woman's nature wholly to give herself.—But on the other hand she does not explain anything.—An eminently masculine intellectuality joined to a feminine submissiveness—this is the truly religious."[60]

On the basis of all these quotations, it appears that Kierkegaard's view of man and woman is very closely connected to his carefully worked-out tenet of the three stages of human life—the esthetic, the ethical, and the religious. Thus there can be great differences in individual development among women and among men and between them, and as a result there is the possibility of countless combinations and comparisons in the relations between the two sexes.[61] Under certain conditions, woman can have, for example, a more strongly developed reflection than man and thus be superior to man at precisely the point where man as a rule has his superiority. In such a case woman, too, must needs suffer through the masculine forms of doubt and despair. It is perhaps a frequent phenomenon in our very reflective age, but nevertheless such instances are exceptions to the rule. One of the pseudonyms says of this whole complex of issues: "I am far from denying that women may have forms of masculine despair and conversely that men may have forms of feminine despair—but these are exceptions. And of course the ideal is also a rarity, and only

---

[59] *JP* VI 6531 (X² A 193).

[60] *JP* IV 5006 (XI² A 70).

[61] Compare with this: ". . . because the exuberant growth of the spiritual life is not inferior to that of nature, and the varieties of the spiritual state are more numerous than those of the flowers." *The Concept of Anxiety*, p. 127 (*SV* IV 394).

ideally is this distinction between masculine and feminine despair altogether true."[62]

We could be tempted to conclude at this point, because the Søren Kierkegaard we meet in the last years of his life speaks of woman, and also of pastors and the Church, with a completely different accent. His statements are bitingly sarcastic and often violent. Some have tried to explain this changed attitude by maintaining that it was something pathological that asserted itself in the last period of his life. However, it must be termed a far too easy solution to make that kind of decision about someone whose opinions in one way or another begin to be disturbing. Therefore I will attempt to give a more simple and fair explanation. Some years ago I discussed Kierkegaard's attack on the church[63] and therefore will only very briefly state here that he felt duty-bound to direct an attack at the Church because the Danish-Lutheran version of Christianity seemed to him to be far too idyllic, entirely too cozy and too comfortable, to have any similarity to the ideals of Christianity as he understood them. Here, therefore, we will look at only his statements about woman and man in this period.

One may ask how he could write in his journals, which he did anticipate would be published at some time, such statements as: "Sexuality is not merely ambiguous in that it can be looked at in two ways, but it can be looked at in a hundred different ways, and there is always a bit of a lie; it is something hidden, which precisely for that reason is extremely dangerous, built entirely on a lie, and woman's element is also a lie."[64] Or one may wonder how he could express himself so ironically and negatively about marriage and motherhood. It is, after all, a big leap from a statement such as "of 100 men who go astray in the world, 99 are saved by women"[65] and to say that by marriage man "is essentially lost for everything higher," or that "getting involved with the other sex is the demotion of man."[66] My simple explanation is this: in the last period of his life, Kierkegaard looked at everything from an extreme Christian point of view, consequently as one who in his thinking and in his life earnestly tried to

---

[62] *The Sickness unto Death*, p. 49 fn. (*SV* XI 162).

[63] G. Malantschuk and N. H. Søe, *Søren Kierkegaards Kamp mod Kirken* (Copenhagen, 1956).

[64] *JP* IV 3970 (XI² A 202).

[65] *Either/Or*, II, p. 211 (ed. tr.) (*SV* II 186).

[66] *JP* IV 5000 (XI¹ A 226).

break with this world. Seen from what to him was the highest existential position, the whole earthly enterprise looks different than when one feels altogether bound to it, and much of what is lauded appears petty and wretched and has to be repudiated.

For the man who wants to withdraw from the world, woman is the power that can tempt him most strongly to return to the earthly relationships, and this he has to guard himself against. In other words, Kierkegaard agrees with the theologian and historian Johannes V. Müller "that there are two great powers around which all revolves: ideas and women."[67] Woman is eager to help man and to make life more pleasant for him, but precisely this can become a temptation for the man who wants to live according to high Christian ideals. As early as *Practice in Christianity*, there is a humorous allusion to this danger. A wife tries in the following manner to calm down her husband, who feels prompted to serve Christianity more strenuously:

> What, do you want to expose yourself to all those annoyances and efforts, and all that ingratitude and opposition? No, let us two enjoy life in coziness and comfort. After all, marriage, as the pastor says, is a state pleasing to God, indeed, the only state of which this is expressly said; it is not even said of the holy orders. We are supposed to get married. God asks nothing more and nothing else of any human being; on the contrary, it is the highest. And you have done enough, you have God's approval, you have gotten married—as a matter of fact, twice. So give up these ideas, they are nothing but vanity and foolishness anyway; the teaching that aims to rip a person out into the world in this way is misanthropic and in no way resembles the Christianity that the pastor on Sunday called the gentle doctrine that amiably relieves all stress. How can you think for one moment that this is supposed to be Christianity, this invention of some sallow, grumbling, misanthropic hermits who have no sense for the feminine.[68]

But it is precisely from this plane of the solitary hermit that Kierkegaard now looks not only at pastors but also at woman. Thus marriage and woman are understood as a hindrance to the person who absolutely wills to seek to live according to what Kierkegaard calls "the ultimate of an ideality."[69]

But, of course, woman as well can choose to renounce the world, and Kierkegaard adheres to the view that in this case woman has to

---

[67] *JP* II 1832 (XI¹ A 288).

[68] *Practice [Training] in Christianity* (Princeton: Princeton University Press, 1941), p. 119 (ed. tr.) (*SV* XII 111-12).

[69] Ibid., p. 7 (ed. tr.) (*SV* XII vii).

sacrifice even more than man: ". . . the Church has laid more emphasis upon the preservation of the woman's virginity than upon the man's and has honored the nun more than the monk, for the woman gives up more than the man when she renounces this life and marriage."[70]

But if Kierkegaard was sharp with pastors and woman, he was no less sharp with man. He calls men "weaklings and globs of spit," because they have lost the relation to the ideal and because they turn away from Christianity "with a certain pride and egotism" as if it were "something for women and children."[71] As a matter of fact, Kierkegaard during these years attacked man more violently than he attacked woman, without a doubt from the position that it is man first and foremost who has been the betrayer in the present state of culture. Judge William already makes this charge against men when he says: "the offense always proceeds from the men; for the man is proud, he wants to be all in all, wants nothing over him."[72]

As previously mentioned, Kierkegaard in the last period of his life takes the Christian ideals to their most extreme logical conclusion. But this does not mean that a person is supposed to begin with this last level and try to fulfill this highest demand in his life; one is supposed to begin at the level where one existentially finds himself to be. Ideals are supposed to stand as a testimony to the difficulties and the struggle to which the single individual will be exposed on the final and crucial level of existence; but at the same time they are supposed to get the rest of us to humble ourselves under them.

If, therefore, one wishes to state Kierkegaard's real view of man and woman, one must stick to the points of view he expressed prior to the attack on the Church, and indeed he himself seems to do this.[73] His conception is mainly based on Christianity's perception of the two sexes as essentially equal without thereby denying that there are sexual differences, which pose particular tasks in life for each of the

---

[70] *JP* IV 4998 (XI¹ A 141).

[71] *JP* IV 5007 (XI² A 192). With regard to "globs of spit," see Revelation 3:16: "So, because you are lukewarm and neither cold nor hot, I will spew you out of my mouth."

[72] *Either/Or*, II, p. 54 (ed. tr.) (*SV* II, 49).

[73] In March 1855, Kierkegaard wrote: "Now I am speaking out far more decisively, frankly, truthfully, without thereby declaring that what I said earlier was untrue." *Judge for Yourselves!* (Princeton: Princeton University Press, 1968), p. 221 (ed. tr.) (*SV* XII 481). See also *Attack on Christendom* (Princeton: Princeton University Press, 1968), p. 52 (*SV* XIV 77); cf. *JP* II 6882 (XI¹ A 210); *Papirer* X⁶ B 115.

sexes. Therefore Kierkegaard resists the attempts to establish sexual equality in the external, secular sense. He has not said much about the particular external tasks man and woman can have over and beyond the traditional ones, but to a certain extent this can always be attributed to his view of the psychical and spiritual difference between the sexes. Yet in Kierkegaard's works we have two examples of his recognizing women who have performed achievements far beyond the ordinary. The one, Madame Thomasine Gyllembourg, was influential through her book *To Tidsaldre* in providing Kierkegaard with the background and the motivation for the penetrating analysis of our confused age that he provides in *Two Ages*. The second, Johanne Luise Heiberg, is eulogized in a little book *The Crisis and a Crisis in the Life of an Actress* for her fine performances as an actress.

As we indicated earlier, Kierkegaard believed that it will never be possible to implement the principle of human equality, and this applies to all the secular areas of life, "even if this struggle were continued for millenia."[74] It hinges on the fact that this world's "nature is diversity,"[75] which will continue as long as the world lasts. This does not, however, preclude a constant striving for greater justice in relations among people, and, as far as the relation between man and woman is concerned, it is most important that they learn to appreciate each other and respect the special characteristics each has received, not only as gift but also as task.

---

[74] *Works of Love*, p. 82 (*SV* IX 73).
[75] *The Point of View*, p. 107 (ed. tr.) (*SV* XIII 589).

4

Assumptions and
Perspectives

Concerning the year of his birth, Kierkegaard half jestingly wrote: "I was born in 1813, in that bad fiscal year when so many other bad banknotes were put in circulation, and my life seems most comparable to one of them. There is a suggestion of greatness in me, but because of the bad conditions of the times I am not worth very much."[1]

Kierkegaard declares that during his childhood and adolescence his father had the most decisive influence on his intellectual-spiritual development. In one place he writes: "I am indebted to my father for everything from the very beginning."[2] In what did this influence consist? In one of his journal entries Kierkegaard says of his childhood: ". . . religiously understood, I was pre-pledged [for-lovet] early in childhood."[3] In these words we have the key to an understanding of Kierkegaard's life. Just as Abraham in the Old Testament was willing to sacrifice his son Isaac, the old Kierkegaard was willing to sacrifice the "son of his old age"[4] by seeking through his upbringing to take away his desire for the life of immediacy and to prepare

[1] *JP* V 5725 (V A 3).
[2] *JP* VI 6164 (IX A 68); see also *Postscript*, p. 553 (*SV* VII 548).
[3] *JP* VI 6389 (X[1] A 272); *JP* VI 6332 (X[5] B 153).
[4] *JP* V 5913 (VII[1] A 126).

him for a special service to Christianity. This sacrifice is the most significant factor in Kierkegaard's life, something which, out of respect for his father, he would never speak about directly. But in a journal entry in 1843, with reference to "Abraham's Collision," he says: "He who has explained this riddle has explained my life."[5] This fact is central in Kierkegaard's life. His own attempt later to sacrifice his betrothed, Regine Olsen, was but a result of the first sacrifice.

In later journal entries, Kierkegaard speaks somewhat more openly of this sacrifice. He writes, for example, of the Isaac who understood that he was going to be sacrificed and thereby himself became an old man just like his father. How early Kierkegaard himself arrived at this understanding is evident in the following statement in the journal: "Inclined to melancholy, given to irony, I recognized that in suffering I had been an old man at the age of eight."[6] This is why the keynote of his childhood and youth became the conviction that he could never be happy as other children and as other young people were. Kierkegaard later struggled to clarify for himself what concrete meaning sacrifice should have for him.

It is remarkable, moreover, that this same father tried to further the development of the very faculties that were most useful to Kierkegaard as thinker and author and that he himself valued most highly. In an indubitably autobiographical portrait, one of Kierkegaard's pseudonyms, Johannes Climacus, tells how his father developed two faculties within him: imagination and dialectic. In this context imagination must be understood especially as the capacity to identify with the lives and life-situations of others, while dialectic means the capacity to think clearly and logically about a specific subject.

Climacus tells how his father, instead of going for a walk with his son out in the city, walks up and down the floor with him, and how they experience in imagination all the places they could think of going to and all the people they could possibly meet. There is something symbolic in this. The father shuts his son away from the actual world but awakens his sentient being to the imaginative creation of a poetized world. In this way "life in his paternal home contributed to the development of his imagination."[7]

---

[5] *JP* V 5640 (IV A 76).

[6] *JP* VI 6379 (X[1] A 234); with regard to the whole question of sacrifice, see especially *JP* II 2223 (X[5] A 132).

[7] *Papirer* IV B 1; *Johannes Climacus or De omnibus dubitandum est* (London: Black, 1958), p. 106 (ed. tr.) (IV B 1, p. 107).

The son learned dialectic in his father's house by listening with the greatest interest to the discussions carried on there, in which his father distinguished himself by his clear and irrefutable argumentation.

These two aspects of Kierkegaard's upbringing had the effect that already as a child he learned how to use his imagination to formulate themes for thought and how to use dialectic to master them. Thus as a child he "had learned to play with that which was to be the serious business of his life."[8]

His father's life and mental depression provided rich material for Kierkegaard's imagination and thinking. He pondered a great deal over the cause of this depression and gradually came to realize that there were certain dark incidents in his father's early life that tormented him. His presentiments of these things prepared the ground for his revolt against his father, but since Kierkegaard had the greatest respect for his father, he continued to respect his strict upbringing.

Kierkegaard enrolled at the University of Copenhagen in 1830; five years later began the rebellion against his father. At that time he discovered beyond a doubt that his father, who had set before him while he was still a child the severe demands of Christianity, had himself been weak at certain crucial points in his life, and that his father was not the man of character he as a child had believed him to be. Because of his father's transgressions, there must be a curse upon the whole family. Kierkegaard called this discovery "the great earthquake,"[9] for through it he came to know the dark side of his father's life and to have a presentiment of the consequences his father's guilt could have for the family.

Kierkegaard now tried to emancipate himself from his previous milieu by living his life as he pleased. Inwardly he was in despair; outwardly he played the role of a happy-go-lucky youth. This eventuated in a temporary break with his father, and he moved away from home in September 1837. Early in 1838, however, there was a reconciliation between father and son.

The previous years, beginning in the autumn of 1835, certainly were the darkest in Kierkegaard's life, but it was precisely in those years that he applied himself most intensely to the important question

---

[8] *Johannes Climacus*, p. 108 (IV B 1, p. 109).
[9] *JP* V 5430 (II A 805).

of understanding himself and the meaning of his existence. With this goal in mind, he pursued very comprehensive independent studies, especially in literature, philosophy, and theology. During this time he gradually realized that his deep despair could be conquered only by faith, the faith from which he was fleeing. He experienced a religious awakening. He became aware of his own weakness and could now better understand his father. As time went by, it became clear to him that it was out of love that his father had made him so unhappy with his demands and upbringing. He and his father talked things over and came to an understanding. A few months later the elder Kierkegaard died, and his son now felt committed to finish his theological courses, which he had for some years neglected in favour of his private studies.

After his father's death in the summer of 1838, Kierkegaard had a relatively quiet and happy period of a few years, during which he attempted to identify more closely with ordinary, conventional life. He studied for his final examinations, and he made the acquaintance of a young girl, Regine Olsen, with the intention of becoming engaged to her. In the summer of 1840, he took his final theological examination, after which he proposed to Regine and received her "Yes."

But it became immediately clear to him that he had made a mistake. He himself said: ". . . the next day I saw that I had made a mistake."[10] His father, after all, had already "pre-pledged" him; therefore this new engagement with Regine had to be broken and the suffering of separation undergone. Later, Kierkegaard wrote of this relationship: "Ah, I have paid dearly for at one time misinterpreting my life and forgetting—that I was pledged!"[11] The thought of being sacrificed, together with his knowledge of his father's guilt and his own earlier life, became a great stumbling block to engagement and marriage. His life was supposed to be a life of penance and a labour in the service of Christianity. Thus his father's powerful influence forced him to give up realizing the universal and to focus instead on a philosophical and religious authorship.

The breaking of the engagement was just as hard for Kierkegaard as it was for Regine. In order to ease the break for her, he finally had to act the role of a villain toward her. The engagement lasted only a year, but in the course of that year Kierkegaard learned a great deal, primarily about himself, but also about a woman's love and about the relation between man and woman in general.

---

[10] *JP* VI 6472 (X⁵ A 149).
[11] *JP* VI 6389 (X¹ A 272).

Several years later, Kierkegaard wrote of this broken engagement: "When I left her, I chose death—for that very reason I have been able to work so enormously."[12] The authorship he initiated was prodigious. Of course, he did not know whether the whole plan would succeed or not, since he constantly had to struggle with wretched health and because the thought of "becoming a rural pastor"[13] continually confronted him as a possibility. In his first books many incidents from the period of his engagement are interwoven as an indirect communication to Regine of the reason for breaking the engagement and the possibility of an understanding on a higher plane. When Regine became engaged again in 1843, this consideration for her was allowed to lapse, and he could devote himself wholly to his task.

An event that had a disproportionately great significance for Kierkegaard was the attack levelled at him by the satirical gazette "The Corsair." He himself had challenged this paper, but he suffered greatly thereafter from the paper's ridicule of him. Most painful for him was the fact that all those who previously had agreed with him on the paper's corrupting influence now sat silent while he was made a laughingstock in everybody's eyes. The bitter experience of being made to look ludicrous led Kierkegaard to allow an even greater infusion of his understanding of Christianity to come out in his subsequent religious books. The world's opposition to Christianity is emphasized more strongly.

Kierkegaard worked for the renewal of Christianity and expected an admission [Indrømmelse] on the part of the church leaders that such a renewal was needed and that the distance from true Christianity was great. When no admission was forthcoming, he launched his violent attack on the established Church[14] in December 1854, on a specific occasion that will not be discussed here since it would take us too far afield. He died November 11, 1855, after presumably having said his last word in this matter.

Søren Kierkegaard's authorship has two parallel sides. The one side consists of the journal entries, which he began in the spring of 1834 and continued until his death. These journal entries can be

---

[12] JP V 5999 (VIII¹ A 100).

[13] The idea of becoming a rural pastor is discussed many places in the journals; here only two will be mentioned: JP 6227 (IX A 213); Papirer X⁵ B 201, p. 382.

[14] For the attack on the established Church, see, for example, G. Malantschuk and N. H. Søe, Søren Kierkegaards Kamp mod Kirken (Copenhagen, 1956).

regarded as "practising in the wings" prior to the public literary undertaking. Kierkegaard did, however, intend that these entries be published sometime after his death. From the very beginning, his writing in the journals was more extensive than his published works.

The other side consists of his public literary works, the first of which appeared in the autumn of 1834 in the form of newspaper articles. In 1838 he published his first book, *From the Papers of One Still Living*. In 1841, his doctoral dissertation, *The Concept of Irony*, was published.

Well prepared, then, Kierkegaard began his authorship proper with the publication of *Either/Or* in 1843. The work came as a huge surprise to the Danish public. The Danish poet and leading critic, J. L. Heiberg, wrote in his review of this book: "And so in these days, like a lightning bolt out of a clear sky, a monster of a book has suddenly plunged down into our reading public; I mean the two big, thick volumes of 54 full, compactly printed sheets [*Ark*] that comprise *Either-Or* by 'Victor Eremita.' "[15]

Kierkegaard's thorough preparation through his "practising in the wings" enabled him (under various pseudonyms) to hurl, in quick succession, more "lightning bolts" down into the Danish reading public. The upbuilding literature that came out concurrently with the pseudonymous works was published under his own name. Thus, in the course of a few years, Kierkegaard provided Danish intellectual life with an enormous and distinctive literature, filled with new and epoch-making ideas.

Kierkegaard realized, however, that there was no contemporary who had the desire and the capacity to grasp the meaning of his authorship. On this point he wrote in 1848: "In such a little country, how would I dare count on a contemporary who had the qualifications and also the time to digest such a deliberately crafty productivity?"[16] That Kierkegaard's opinion was correct can best be seen from the very superficial comments on the authorship made by one of the best representatives of philosophic and theological training in Denmark at that time, the subsequent Bishop H. L. Martensen, in the introduction to his book on dogmatics published in 1849. He considered Kierkegaard to be one of those who lacked the "initiative for cohe-

---

[15] *Intelligensblade*, no. 24 (March 1, 1843), p. 288. Cf. *Papirer* IV B 104.

[16] *The Point of View*, p. 85 fn. (ed. tr.) (*SV* XIII 570). Kierkegaard's attempt to introduce Professor Rasmus Nielsen to his new ideas is a chapter of its own. On that subject, see especially *JP* VI 6403-06 (X⁶ B 83-102).

rent, systematic thinking but was satisfied to think in aphorisms and apothegms, in caprices and flashes . . . .[17]

In 1848, in *The Point of View for My Work as an Author*, Kierkegaard sought to explain what he was aiming at in his writing. But the book ended up with so much information of a personal and more intimate nature that he decided it should not be published until after his death. However, in order to make public a direct communication about his authorship, he published in 1851 the very condensed little book *On My Work as an Author*. These two books are extremely significant for the understanding of Kierkegaard's life and authorship because they contain many fine autobiographical features and much literary information about the relations of the various books to each other.[18] Moreover, while working on the books just mentioned, Kierkegaard gave more thought to the future and to world history than he had previously. At first he was negatively disposed toward such reflections—presumably, for one thing, because of his opposition to Grundtvig. But at this point, when he was practically finished with his authorship proper and was trying to assess its place and significance in the future, it was easy for him to engage also in world-historical reflections.

But on the whole, it must first be mentioned that Kierkegaard considered that he had advanced many new ideas in his authorship. Alluding to the two books, *The Sickness unto Death* and *Practice in Christianity*, he says that they contain a "wealth of ideas."[19]

Kierkegaard was primarily a great philosophical anthropologist, and he provides many new insights into the nature of man and human existence. He fathomed himself and others imaginatively and succeeded in describing the psychical and spiritual development of the human person on all its levels and in all its valleys and abysses. In this respect, his works can be placed side by side with Dostoevsky's profound delineations of man—with this one difference, that Kierkegaard had a clearer comprehension of the powers constituting and governing man.

Kierkegaard's unique insight into the question of human freedom and human responsibility made it possible for him to develop this doctrine of the stages in man's spiritual development and their inter-

---

[17] H. Martensen, *Den christelige Dogmatik* (Copenhagen, 1849), p. III.

[18] For more on Kierkegaard's use of literary forms, see F. J. Billeskov Jansen, *Studier i Søren Kierkegaards litterære Kunst* (Copenhagen, 1951).

[19] *JP* VI 6238 (IX A 227).

connectedness. The point of departure for all his reflections on man is the premise that man is a synthesis of two opposite qualities: the transient and the eternal.

In addition to this, Kierkegaard's great service is that on the basis of his doctrine of the stages he clearly distinguishes the sphere of knowledge from the sphere of faith. Influenced by Hegelian philosophy, there was a tendency in Kierkegaard's time to place knowledge higher than faith. But Kierkegaard points out carefully and conclusively that there are a content and a correlation to which scientific knowledge and scholarship are unequal; they belong to the sphere of faith. Seen from the side of logical thought, these correlations must be designated as containing a contradiction and thus are paradoxical and absurd; but they are no less a reality, even though they are outside the confines of scientific knowledge and scholarship. Thus, Kierkegaard once again puts faith in first place.

In this connection, Kierkegaard's authorship provides totally new definitions of faith as a whole and, above all, of the faith that belongs to Christianity and is built upon the conviction that the eternal truth has been revealed in a particular historical person.

In connection with the affirmation that Christianity is the revelation of the eternal truth in historical time, Kierkegaard advances subtle and penetrating analyses of the concept of the historical itself. Certainly one of the most important results of these analyses is his demonstration that no historical-critical, scientific view of the New Testament can ever have any decisive meaning for Christian faith.[20]

According to Kierkegaard, the most important of the new views he advanced in relation to Christianity was the idea of "the situation of contemporaneity"—that is, the idea that every person should test himself as to how he would relate to Christ if he were his contemporary. The great importance Kierkegaard attributed to this thought is seen in the following entry: "Out with history. In with the situation of contemporaneity. . . . This is really the direction in which my whole productivity has tended."[21] Only through the situation of contemporaneity does a person learn that there is no way to truth without colliding with the possibility of offence.

---

[20] On this, see G. Malantschuk, "*Søren Kierkegaards Modifikationer af det kristelige,*" *Dansk Teol. Tidsskrift*, XX (1957), 228.

[21] *JP* I 691 (IX A 95); see also *Attack upon Christendom*, p. 242 (*SV* XIV 300). This whole question is treated in detail in Per Lønning, *Samtidighedens Situation* (Oslo, 1954).

Kierkegaard has also very thoroughly delineated all the conditions in man that develop as an expression of the absence of faith. To these belong anxiety, despair, and offence. Note that all these negative conditions are described by someone who has himself lived through them.

To Kierkegaard's new and original ideas belong also his working out of the category of "the single individual." He was convinced that his "possible ethical significance"[22] in the future was "unconditionally" linked to the thoughts and reflections he had advanced with respect to "the single individual." It comes out clearly in the following words: ". . . my whole thought activity as author is focused in this one idea, 'the single individual,' the category that will prove to be the *point de vue* of the future, the category the significance of which (politically, ethically, religiously) the future will more and more make manifest."[23]

With the expression "the single individual," Kierkegaard wanted primarily to stress the eternal worth of the individual person. This viewpoint is linked to his conception of man as a synthesis of time and eternity, a conception that according to Kierkegaard explains all the incompatibilities and idiosyncrasies in human nature. This understanding is closely linked to faith in a conscious power behind the course of the world. The individual person's worth is determined by what is assumed to be the ultimate ground of existence. Indeed, history shows us that every time the idea of God is undermined, the worth of the individual person is also diminished.

Kierkegaard demonstrates further that surrendering the thought of God will always result in searching for surrogates for God. Faith in God is replaced with faith in the nation, in the age, in mankind, yes, even in the party—since in this way everyone can become the highest authority. There are many instances in Kierkegaard's writing that point to this consequence of atheism.

The tendency to abolish totally the idea of God and thereby devalue the meaning of the individual person comes especially from the modern natural sciences. Since they have been able to show immense results from their investigation into the visible and empirical world, there is a great temptation for them also to want to make

---

[22] *The Point of View*, p. 129 (ed. tr.) (*SV* XIII 605).
[23] *Papirer* X⁵ B 247; cf. *JP* II 2021 (X⁵ B 244). With regard to Kierkegaard's views on the category "the single individual" in relation to community, see Valter Lindström, *Efterföljelsens teologi hos Søren Kierkegaard* (Stockholm, 1956).

pronouncements about existence as a whole. It is implicit in the nature of the case that the natural sciences as exact sciences are obliged to stop with certain ultimate, material components about which clarification may be sought through experimentation.

But the large question that cannot be answered by way of science still remains—namely, from whence comes the movement that sets the world in motion. Here there are but two possible answers: either there is a conscious power behind the whole thing, or the whole thing has its origin in what Kierkegaard, using a term from Greek philosophy of nature, calls a "vortex." The materialistic natural sciences must consistently choose the latter alternative and thereby crucially influence their view of man.[24]

In these schools of thought, man becomes just a natural product and is thereby reduced to a meaningless and vanishing moment in the great course of the world. Instead of the eternal worth of the individual person, quantitative categories are stressed; "the crowd" and the mass-man with his blind search after surrogates for God come to the fore. For this reason, Kierkegaard sees in the materialistic natural sciences a great danger for the ethical conception of man. This explains his sharp assertion that "*ultimately all corruption will come from the natural sciences.*"[25] The development of these sciences and the mass's admiration of their progress were bound to promote the relativizing of all values and have a disintegrating effect on the ethical norms that have their ground in something eternal. At the same time, men were willing to put their trust in the capability of the natural sciences. Concerning this disposition, Kierkegaard sketched the following perspective: "The conflict between God and 'man' will therefore culminate in the withdrawal of 'man' behind natural science. And it is perhaps the trend of the future that Christianity now wants to shake off illusions, with the result that there will be hosts of people whose religion will become natural science."[26]

This whole movement toward the natural sciences will weaken man's capacity for independent thinking, and since "there are so few

---

[24] All materialistic positions must inevitably end with a kind of belief in "vortex" as "the world's central principle." This very widespread belief is found in numerous elaborations in modern times. Most familiar is the form found in Friedrich Engels, *Dialectics of Nature* (New York: International Publishers, 1940).

[25] *JP* III 2809 (VII^1 A 186).

[26] *JP* III 2823 (X^5 A 73).

dialecticians in each generation, and there will be fewer—then natural science will harness all mankind.''[27]

Kierkegaard points out in many places and in many ways the weaknesses of the materialistic view. He can, for example, ironize over the notion that tremendous external progress will have essential significance for ethical and spiritual development of persons. He also points out the inconsistency in materialistic biology, which to him is comic when it believes that it can "find the spirit which gives life"[28] after having first put it to death.

The strongest argument against materialistic biology, however, is that despite all its comprehensive descriptions and cataloguing, it can explain nothing. On the basis of research and experience it can describe phenomena, but it cannot explain what is most important: the transition from the one level to the next. This transition is a leap—indeed, according to Kierkegaard, it is a constant miracle. The self-contradiction in these materialistic views is, among other things, that the very ones who contend against miracle are the very ones who tacitly assume it. How can they otherwise explain the appearance in the human being of a psychical world with its own laws that cannot be derived simply from the movements of atoms. Moreover, it is naive to explain development by eons of time alone; a nothing cannot become something merely through the length of time. If the natural scientists venture beyond empirical data with their explanations, their enterprise ends in mythology, but a mythology inferior to what they think they find in the Bible's ancient narratives.

Kierkegaard's authorship contains a "science of arms" against all the levelling trends mentioned, regardless of what they are called. At the same time, he provides a positive solution through a careful explication of the paths along which the human individual becomes "the single individual," which according to Kierkegaard is the highest goal for a human being. He saw it as his task in a confused age to be a guide into the future. He says of himself that he is "a presentient figure, who has discerned with categorical correctness the future of history, the turn that has to be made and that will become the future of history."[29]

In this as in other journal entries, Kierkegaard manifests his faith that his view of man will ultimately be victorious. The "turn" of

[27] *JP* III 2816 (VII¹ A 196).
[28] *JP* III 2809 (VII¹ A 186).
[29] *Papirer* IX B 64.

which he speaks means primarily the renewed consolidation of faith in man's eternal worth.

But before this happens there will be a time of catastrophes, already heralded by the revolutionary movements in 1848. In this "age of disintegration," man will try to solve his existential problems by means of his own powers and understanding. It will cost "sufferings and bloodshed,"[30] until the insight that only eternity can solve all the human problems once again blazes the trail.

Kierkegaard also believed that initially the modern atheistic movements would make their appearance as political trends but eventually would manifest that their deepest incentive was religious in nature. On this point he writes: "The future will correspond inversely to the Reformation: then everything appeared to be a religious movement and became politics; now everything appears to be politics but will become a religious movement."[31] Kierkegaard, however, believed that in our age the upheaval would be radical in a way totally different from the upheaval at the time of the Reformation. In a journal entry, he even compares our age to the situation at the time of Christ, declaring that our age "almost resembles the moment when Christianity made its appearance in the world."[32]

According to Kierkegaard, the zeal with which a political movement tries to fight the idea of God is not merely a sign of the depth of the demonic in the movement but also a proof of man's intense need for the eternal.

In his criticism of political movements, Kierkegaard's emphasis on the significance of the eternal must not be construed as a defence of the errors which some of these movements accuse Christendom of having. After all, in his own attack on Christendom, he demonstrated that he, too, could see its errors. Everything considered, his criticism focuses on something more central: with his accent on the eternal he wanted to point out that, looked at most deeply, no one can avoid a relation to it; the eternal will make its claim either positively or negatively. To this must be added that in Kierkegaard's opinion the deepest basis for a person's turning away from the eternal or from God is in willing more than in knowing. The believer has no need whatsoever to be more intellectually developed than the doubter or

---

[30] *Papirer* IX B 10.
[31] *JP* VI 6255 (IX B 63:7), 6256 (X⁶ B 40).
[32] *Papirer* X⁵ B 205.

the atheist. Everything depends on one's willingness to perceive the limits of his knowing and on one's ability to learn to obey the eternal. But this is the very sector where the difficulties lie. Modern man refuses to acknowledge the validity of the eternal demand and wants to be his own lord and master.

For this reason, Kierkegaard, with some justification, can call the modern levelling movements a mutiny against God. He foresaw the possibility of an organized mutiny, in which "the crowd" would be "fitted out in boots"[33] and exploited for purposes of which it had no comprehension. The world has seen mass-men's organized mutiny against God take two forms: "the proletarian rebellion" with Marx and "the aristocratic rebellion" with Nietzsche as theoreticians.

Some thinkers in modern philosophy have attempted to undergird with "ethical" arguments this formula of despair and maintain that the battle against God is to be regarded as something good and meritorious. Contrary to the philosopher Kant, who maintained that in order to give a ground for ethical norms the existence of God had to be postulated, the eminent modern thinker Nicolai Hartmann, for example, believes that the existence of God has to be denied, for otherwise it will endanger man as a moral and ethical being.[34] With this, Hartmann's so-called "postulatory atheism," the opposition to the idea of God analyzed by Kierkegaard has reached its ultimate. It is impossible to go any further in denying the existence of God. This reasoning, inspired by Nietzsche, manifests the same weaknesses as the atheism oriented to the natural sciences, since they have a kindred view of the world's ultimate ground. In one way, what Kierkegaard said about Hegelian philosophy, that one attempts "to sew without fastening the end and without tying a knot in the thread,"[35] applies to both these movements.

Kierkegaard did not doubt that Christianity would have the final word in the great battle about the new view of man. He worked with unconditioned confidence in his analysis, a confidence primarily based on the conviction that Christianity alone is able to give a solution to all the existential problems. For this reason he also pins his hope for the future on "the single individual" who submits himself in

---

[33] *Papirer* IX B 24, p. 326.

[34] On this, see Nicolai Hartmann, *Ethics*, I-III (London: Allen & Unwin, 1932); *Teleologisches Denken* (Berlin, 1951).

[35] *The Sickness unto Death*, p. 93 (*SV* XI 204); cf. *JP* III 3540 (XI² A 281), 3689 (X⁴ A 190); *The Point of View*, p. 158 (*SV* XIII 508); *Attack*, p. 113 (*SV* XIV 138).

total obedience to the demand and the invitation of Christianity. On this point he writes in *The Point of View for My Work as an Author*:

> . . . for I certainly do have faith in the rightness of my thought in the face of the whole world, but the next to the last thought I would give up is my faith in individuals. And this is my faith—that however much confusion and evil and abomination there may be in people as soon as they get to be the irresponsible and impenitent "public," "the crowd," etc., there is just as much that is true, good, and kind in them if one can get them to be individuals. Oh, what human beings, what lovable human beings they could become if they would become individuals before God![36]

---

[36] *The Point of View*, p. 158 (ed. tr.) (*SV* XIII 499).

5

Did Kierkegaard Read
Karl Marx?

Although Søren Kierkegaard and Karl Marx lived and worked in the same decades in Europe, defended their doctoral dissertations the same year (1841), and began their literary activity about the same time, they did not—as far as one is able to ascertain—know each other. As far as Kierkegaard is concerned, at least, there is no mention of Marx either in his works or in his journals; this does not preclude, however, the possibility that he encountered Marx's name in *Kjøbenhavnsposten*.[1] But it is interesting that Kierkegaard may be presumed to have read in a book entitled *Anekdota* and published by Arnold Ruge a short article by *Kein Berliner*, a pseudonym that concealed the name Karl Marx, which fact Kierkegaard of course could not know. The article has the heading *"Luther als Schiedsrichter zwischen Strauss und Feuerbach."*[2]

The background for Marx's article is the discussion created by two of Hegel's disciples, Friedrich Strauss and Ludwig Feuerbach, on the basis of their books *Das Leben Jesu* (1835-36) and *Das Wesen des Christenthums* (1841). These two authors, each from his own

---

[1] See Svend E. Stybe, *Frederik Dreier* (Copenhagen, 1959), p. 97.

[2] *Anekdota zur neuesten deutschen Philosophie und Publicistik, herausgegeben von Arnold Ruge*, I-II (Zürich, 1843; *ASKB* 753). "Luther as Judge between Strauss and Feuerbach," *Karl Marx Early Texts*, pp. 23-25.

point of departure, attempted to continue and intensify the trend in Hegel's system—namely, to degrade Christianity in relation to philosophy and scientific knowledge. With his historical-critical method, Strauss, for example, tried to demonstrate the mythological character of Christianity, while Feuerbach argued that the Christian faith could be fully explained on the basis of man's anthropological presuppositions. As time went on, Marx eagerly joined the endeavour—his objective was to adapt the elements in Hegel's idealistic philosophy to a materialistic view of life. Here Strauss's speculative theology was quite useless, but he seized with interest Feuerbach's interpretation of Christ's resurrection in his book *Das Wesen des Christenthums*. In his critique of Hegel's idealistic abstract system, Marx's primary aim was to find another and more solid foundation for philosophy, and he stopped initially at material and economic actualities as the genuine and indisputable basis for all relations in existence. He then attempted to build his philosophy and social doctrine upon this. Here Feuerbach's endeavour to explain the origin of religion by way of anthropology became a welcome assistance. Indeed, Feuerbach felt that he was able to prove that all religious and spiritual conceptions human beings have about life and existence arise out of men's egotistic desires and longings and their need to create for themselves an imaginary, loftier scheme of things. Marx builds further on these presuppositions, yet with the understanding that the driving power behind the formation of all social, intellectual, and religious ideas is unsatisfied material and economic needs. Therefore, Engels was entirely correct when some time later he declared that in many respects Feuerbach became a connecting link between Hegelian philosophy and Marx's and Engels' philosophy.[3]

What also clearly appealed to Marx in Feuerbach was that he did not distort Christianity but represented it in its true form, in all its contrast to universally human existence, and did it in such a way that his description acted as profound irony against current, secularized Christianity. That Feuerbach was right in his representation of Christianity as opposed to Strauss, who wanted to turn Christianity into mythology, was confirmed for Marx in Luther, whom Marx therefore invokes as judge in the conflict between the two. The specific, concrete occasion for this conflict, in which Marx involves himself in this article, was the question of the reality of miracle in Christianity.

---

[3] See Friedrich Engels, "Foreword," *Ludwig Feuerbach and the Outcome of Classical German Philosophy* (London: Lawrence & Wishart, 1941), pp. 15-16.

Strauss denies that miracles can take place, while Feuerbach acknowledges them inasmuch as miracles become a reality for people if they believe in them. In his article, Marx aligns himself with Feuerbach's view and sharply criticizes Strauss, who he feels is still looking at these matters as they looked to the eyes of speculative theology. Feuerbach, however, is praised for "making short work of it" by declaring that "miracle is the realization of a natural or human wish in a supernatural manner."[4]

That miracle is regarded as a reality in Christianity, Marx finds confirmed in Luther in one of his discourses on the resurrection of the dead (Luke 7). By citing various passages, Marx shows that here Luther directly provides "an *apology* for the whole Feuerbachian work—an apology for the definitions of *providence, omnipotence, creation, miracle, faith* as they are given in this work."[5] And Marx concludes:

> Oh, shame on you, you Christians, *shame on you* that an Anti-Christ has to show you the nature of Christianity in its true, undisguised form! And you, you speculative theologians and philosophers, I advise you to extricate yourselves from the concepts and biases of hitherto speculative philosophy if you have any desire at all to come to things as they are—that is, to *the truth*. And there is no other way for you to *truth* and *freedom* than *through Fire-Brook*.[6] Feuerbach is the present age's purgatory.[7]

The remarkable aspect of this conclusion is Marx's advice to Christians to learn from the atheist Feuerbach what true Christianity is; but at the same time he also counsels the speculative theologians and philosophers not to bypass Feuerbach's representation of Christianity but on the contrary to go through this "Feuer-bach" in order thereby to free themselves from a philosophy which, according to Marx, was still built upon elements of the Christian view of life. Only through such a cleansing process would philosophy be able to come "to truth and freedom." In saying this, Marx is actually directing his scorn at both camps. First at the Christians, who do not know what Christianity is, and then at speculative theologians and philosophers, who do not know what philosophy's task is. As for Marx's own

---

[4] *Anekdota*, p. 206.

[5] Ludwig Feuerbach, *Das Wesen des Christenthums* (2d ed.; Leipzig, 1843; *ASKB* 488); *The Essence of Christianity* (New York: Harper, 1957).

[6] *Feuer-bach*.

[7] *Anekdota*, p. 208.

position, this is not immediately clear from the contents of the article; on the first reading one will be inclined to interpret it as being very positive in relation to Christianity.

But before proceeding further, the question whether Kierkegaard actually read this article needs to be answered. In my opinion, the following reasons leave no doubt of it. In 1844 in a note to *Philosophical Fragments*, Kierkegaard wrote that he had read in *Anekdota* a discussion of Feuerbach by Ruge.[8] It is inconceivable that when he read Ruge's review he was not aware of *Kein Berliner*'s brief article with the exciting title. That this was the case is apparent in the fact that Kierkegaard in the above-mentioned entry where he refers to Ruge's review of Feuerbach's book divides Feuerbach's name into two parts so that it becomes "Fire Brook." Kierkegaard's journal entry reads: "Feuerbach nevertheless is consistent and illuminates by his contrasts; this does not mean, however, that one has to go through that Fire Brook. (See *Anekdota* by Ruge, an article written by him)." But this separating of the name appears at the end of the article by *Kein Berliner*, *not* in Ruge's review.

Consequently, Kierkegaard in his journal entry first mentions Feuerbach's consistent, that is, trustworthy, representation of Christianity and then points out that Feuerbach became its opponent. However, Kierkegaard does not believe that one needs go to an opponent of Christianity to find out what Christianity is (consequently go through a "Fire Brook"), and Feuerbach's insight into the gist of Christianity actually did not, after all, lead him to a positive relation to it but to offence. Thus he becomes a clear example of the choice a person has to make between faith and offence, whereas Hegel's "mediation effort" obliterates the possibility of offence. In a second note to *Philosophical Fragments*, Kierkegaard sketchily says on this point: "Feuerbach's indirect service to Christianity as an *offended* individuality, the illusion it takes in our age to become offended since Christianity has been made as mild as possible, as meaningless as the scrawl a physician makes at the top of the prescription. —The formulation is absolutely correct according to the Hegelian maundering mediation endeavor."[9]

---

[8] *Papirer* V B 1, p. 10. Kierkegaard may have obtained the first detailed information about Feuerbach's *Das Wesen des Christenthums* through Ruge's review. Kierkegaard purchased *Anekdota* February 20, 1844. A month later he got Feuerbach's book.

[9] *Papirer* V B 9.

But even before encountering Feuerbach, Kierkegaard had perceived that a watering down and distortion of Christianity had taken place and that Hegel's philosophy had contributed to this. That was why Kierkegaard, just as did the left-Hegelians Strauss, Feuerbach, and Marx, began his literary activity by taking stock of his relation to Hegel. But while the left-Hegelians, each in his own way, continued Hegel's trend toward a destruction of Christianity, Kierkegaard turned to the central points in Hegel's system—namely, his dialectical method and his attempt to replace Christianity with philosophy. Thereafter, Kierkegaard sought directly and indirectly to develop a view of Christianity that could engage in battle with all the levelling tendencies that followed in the wake of Hegel's philosophy.

Thus, as a consequence of the polemic against Hegel, Kierkegaard was forced to go part of the way along the same road as Feuerbach, consequently through "Fire Brook"—that is, to realize Christianity's bankruptcy in time and to attempt to define its true nature. But while Feuerbach continued to take a negative stance toward Christianity, Kierkegaard placed his whole authorship in the service of Christianity. It is on the basis of this positive relation to Christianity that Kierkegaard takes his position on Strauss and Feuerbach. Kierkegaard did not take very seriously Strauss's attempt to make Christianity mythology, but in order to put an end once and for all to all efforts to cast doubt on the historical truth of Christianity, he has his pseudonym Climacus advance his "world-historical NB." With this, attention is drawn to the fact that from the point of view of history there can never be any doubt that there existed a community ("we") who believed that God had manifested himself in human form and had lived and died as a human being. This, Climacus believes, is more than sufficient as an historical point of departure for Christianity.

Just as for Marx, so also for Kierkegaard, the relation to Feuerbach had a more serious character. Kierkegaard was sympathetic to Feuerbach's depiction of true Christianity and thereby his disclosure that current Christianity was an aberration. Kierkegaard also respected, as we have seen, Feuerbach's being offended by Christianity. But he turns all the more vigorously on Feuerbach's claim that all theology is anthropology. This Feuerbachian point of view must not be confused with Kierkegaard's own view that every human being as a synthesis of the eternal and the temporal has the possibility of the eternal and on that foundation can himself form religious ideas. The great difference is that Kierkegaard believes that Christianity in particular can never be a human invention or creation. In other words, in relation to all human cognition and competence, it is absurd. The fact that later, after Christianity has entered into the world, one can describe it and point out its contradictions, as Feuerbach does, does not prove that it is a human invention. Neither philosophy nor anthropology can ever explain Christianity; at most they can be offended by it, as was Feuerbach. In his two psychological-anthropological works, *The Concept of Anxiety* and *The Sickness unto Death*, Kierkegaard's pseudonyms radically and fittingly reject Feuerbach's claim that Christianity can be explained on the basis of man's anthropological presuppositions. Thus Kierkegaard would never be able to accept Marx's statement on the basis of Feuerbach's anthropology that "man makes religion, religion does not make man."[10] For Kierkegaard, the earnestness lies precisely in the fact that Christianity is able to re-create man.

With regard to Marx's relation to Feuerbach as purgatory (*Purgatorium*), it is, as mentioned, difficult to decide on the basis of his remarks in the short article whether he has a positive or a negative attitude toward Christianity. It is also hard to say anything definite about what Kierkegaard thought of *Kein Berliner*, who so intrepidly quotes Luther. In any case it was clear to him that *Anekdota* leaned toward the left-Hegelian point of view. But anyone who knew the person behind the pseudonym could have no doubt that it was an opponent of Christianity who spoke here.

Marx's conviction that the material and the economic are the only true reality inevitably had to bring him into sharp opposition to a religion that affirms the priority of the spiritual over the material. If materialism tries to abolish the conception of God, the consequence will always be, as Marx expresses it, that "man is the highest being for man,"[11] which is exactly what Feuerbach more pregnantly expressed in the following statement: "*Homo homini Deus est* [Man is God for man]—this is the great practical principle:—this is the axis upon which revolves the history of the world."[12] As sovereign lord, man has the power to arrange everything on earth. According to

---

[10] "Towards a Critique of Hegel's Philosophy of Right," *Karl Marx Early Texts*, p. 115.

[11] Ibid., p. 128.

[12] *The Essence of Christianity*, p. 271. In Nietzsche, as well, we see that the repudiation of God has to end with a deification of man.

Marx, this must take place through class war, whereby economic equality is to be achieved and the "Messianic idea"[13] of a kingdom of justice on earth implemented by the proletariat.

In our day, Marx and Kierkegaard stand as a challenge to the world that has lost the sustaining spiritual foundation of its existence. Each of them has something that attracts and something that repels people. What appeals to many in Marx is his theory that it is economics that forms the basis of all human existence, and his promise that it is possible to build on this foundation a perfect society in which all are equal. This claim for the importance of economics cannot be denied, but it is one-sided if, as Marx does, one merely regards the spiritual side of man as a super-structure, however much is put into it. In contrast to other creatures, man is marked by the spiritual as something fundamental. Moreover, the idea of perfect equality between persons is utopian and can never be carried out in this world, the nature of which is diversity.

Kierkegaard's strength is his profound knowledge of man's interior life and its psychological and anthropological presuppositions. In this sphere, Marx is totally inadequate.[14] Kierkegaard utilizes this knowledge to show that man falls short of his high destiny if he does not let himself be led by the ethical and religious truths of Christianity. What is repelling in Kierkegaard is that he does not merely call attention to Christianity in its true form, as Feuerbach does, but sets it as a goal that neither complies with man's earth-bound desires and demands nor is capable of being reconciled with secularized editions of Christianity.

Kierkegaard and Marx thereby confront man with a challenging Either/Or: he can either stay inside the esthetic sphere with its craving for happiness, with its mundane practical morality and its continual quantitative calculating of ways of getting this happiness—or he can walk the road where the single individual, while performing his responsibilities in this world, is built up and rescued by faith in eternal and unchangeable values.

---

[13] See N. Berdiaev, *Christentum und Klassenkampf* (Zürich, 1936), especially p. 16.

[14] Cf. the following in Johannes Witt-Hansen's fine account in *Historisk Materialisme* (Copenhagen, 1973), p. 30 (ed. tr.): "It is probably fair to say that man's role as a 'social animal' and the activity that he as such develops are not fully taken into account in Marx's anthropology."

A